Conscious Software Development

Jeff McKenna

Illustrated by Diana Lee

Conscious Software Development
by Jeff McKenna

Printing History

August 2014: First Edition (version 1.0)

ISBN-10: 1496011333
ISBN-13: 978-1496011336

I dedicate this book to all those persons who are working to improve the consciousness of their personal lives, in their working lives, and in their everyday activities—mindfully improving how they live. Thank you all.

Contents

Foreword

You are about to have a conversation with someone who has had a quiet but significant influence on modern software development. Jeff won't be telling you about technical practices, designs patterns or architectural models, though. He will be sharing his experiences in the evolution of an industry as a feeling, thinking human being. He does not fit the stereotype of the introverted, insular techno-geek. Nor is he the bragging hero that can be found in diminishing numbers in the industry. Jeff will tell you his stories and give you his opinions with humility from the heart.

For the past few years I have been fortunate to have some of these conversations in real time. Jeff has helped me grow in my own career by being my mentor, friend, sounding board and lunch partner. We meet somewhere in Silicon Valley once a month. He keeps track of whose turn it is to pay. I record the light bulbs that he turns on in my head. If I had a dollar for every time I have told one of my classes something that "my friend Jeff said…" then I could buy lunch every time. Now you get a chance to join in these conversations through this easy-going and thought-provoking volume.

It may surprise you to find a technical craftsperson who can do intense programming and design work and reflect on their personal involvement at the same time. In many corporate environments we are so busy with the technology and impossible deadlines to reflect on our own role in the story. Jeff has been instrumental in changing the industry to a more humane way of working. As coach to the first

Scrum team in 1993, he was part of the discovery and establishment of a more thoughtful and productive way of working now called Agile Software Development. He continues his efforts to bring Agile thinking into the mainstream of industry and a wider world of responsible and human-friendly work culture.

If you are a technical worker, this book will widen your perspective, permit you to pause and give you some great things to think about during the pause. If you are non-technical and curious about being conscious in your work, you will find some useful tips and fresh perspectives from which to reflect on your relationship to work and its place in your life.

Jeff loves what he does. He is about to share that with you.

Roger Brown
Programmer and Agile Coach
San Diego, CA
June 1, 2014

Acknowledgments

Acknowledgments are hard. I want to acknowledge everybody, but I can't quite do that. Well perhaps I can. I acknowledge everyone who has had an impact on my life—which is a lot more people than even I know.

In particular I want to thank my wife, Cory, for her wonderful support and what she has done to help me be more of who I am, and giving me the space and freedom to explore and understand a little bit more about what's in me.

I want to acknowledge the people who helped get this book together: Hillary Johnson, Chris Sims and last, but not least, the person who has really helped me complete it, Steve Bockman. Thank you all very much.

In particular I want to acknowledge the teachers in consciousness I have had the last nine years with the Diamond Approach: Jeanine Mamary, Sherry Ruth Anderson, Vince Draddy, Dale Sides and of course, most of all, Hameed Ali.

On the technical side, I've had many mentors over the years who have helped me. The two people who have helped me the most in becoming who I am as a software person are Ward Cunningham and Kent Beck. Jerry Weinberg helped me discover my heart in the middle of my software life.

Thanks again to all of you people and all others that have influenced and guided me towards living a more conscious life.

Introduction

Let's talk about conscious software development. This book has been some time in the making. I've known about the title for many years now and finally it looks like it's coming together.

We put this book together by my taking some time and recording a number of video sessions that basically became the individual topics that are in this book. Because of this, and how I was thinking about it all along, the book doesn't really have a beginning and an end—a flow from one end to the other. It's more a set of individual topics that cover a wide range of thoughts and ideas and experiences I've had in the last fifty years doing software development.

So in some sense it's a personal story—I tell some stories in the book but mostly it's about what I've learned, how I've distilled those experiences into something that you might call some kind of knowledge or maybe even a little bit of wisdom. I'll let you be the judge of that.

Each topic stands on its own, yet they all talk about consciousness in one form or another, all the different aspects of it, ranging from how we talk together, how we think, how we breathe about it, how we check in with our bodies, how we think about problems, how we debug, how we do what we do.

It's not "do this and it'll get better for you." It's not that kind of book. This isn't a how-to book, except maybe it's a book about stimulus—

it's a way to think about how you do what you do, to get you to contemplate, to do a little inquiry into how you work and what happens for you.

I expect people to read this book—maybe not the whole thing—just a piece at a time, and then to use that as a springboard for a coversation either with yourself, maybe with others, about how you do your work. What does it mean to be a software developer, for you? Because it's more important for you to be who *you* are, not to be who *I* am. (I have enough trouble being myself without having other people trying to be me. That doesn't work so well.)

Hopefully this gives you some idea of what we're looking for in terms of what we're trying to do, what we're trying to convey, with this book.

So welcome. Welcome to this book. Welcome to *Conscious Software Development*. I hope you will use it as a time to think and reflect a little bit. Read it slowly and enjoy it. And let me know what you think.

Have a great day.

—*Jeff McKenna*

Human Driven Development

The soft stuff is the hard stuff

If you are a young software developer, most likely you are used to working by yourself on a computer. You probably enjoy the thrill of solving problems on your own. Many of us in software started our careers working alone and loving it.

But if we are going to solve problems in a commercial context, then we have to learn to get some pleasure out of working together.

Complex systems like software can only be designed and developed by multiple people working together to solve problems, and to do so they have to communicate—with each other and not just with a computer. This is a key message of agile software development, which says, "We can get more done if we work as a team."

But what does that mean for you as an individual? Does that mean that you have to change the way you are? That you must now act differently? It probably does!

Does that mean you have to learn differently? Again the answer is: probably so!

How do you accomplish that? By being conscious about how you work, by thinking about your own processes and your team's processes—and not just the processes of the computer.

Early in my own career, the computer was the centerpiece. I liked nothing better than to just go at a problem and solve it.

As developers, we're naturally inclined to want to do everything all by ourselves. We sit down at a machine, fire up our system, clack out the work product and send it along. The earliest manifestation of any kind of problem is when someone reading the documentation or the code encounters simple errors, things like words missing or exceptions missed.

If typos and glitches were the only ill effects of going it alone, this might not be a very big problem. But working with others is about more than missing words and simple errors of omission. The larger point is that when we work alone we lose the opportunity to help one another become better at what we do.

When I was just getting into the consulting business for myself, I submitted one of my very first proposals to a software project manager who glanced at it and asked me exactly three questions. I answered the first two just fine, but blew the third—I had overlooked a very simple design flaw, and just like that, it was over. I didn't get the contract.

That moment was a wake-up call for me. I learned that just because you work on something and think that you've got it right—that doesn't mean that it is right! I learned that I needed to get help, and not just when a problem arose, but all along the way. When you go it alone, you can fail over the simplest mistakes.

That was the first inkling I had that, "Wait a minute, this Lone Ranger thing is not going to work."

Learning to learn

So now the question becomes, how do I learn how to learn in this new world? To figure it out, I had to understand how I learn. This applies to you—you have to understand how you learn.

Do you read books?

Do you talk to people?

Do you need to try your hand at a thing first, then read about it?

What works for you? What's difficult for you?

Difficult is okay, if it's effective. Easy is okay, too.

Me, I know that I learn better by reading. If I need to learn a new language, I start by reading the entire manual and then solving some problems in the language. I have learned that if I dive right into solving problems with a new technology without an overview; without some big picture, such as reading a manual first, I will struggle.

I learned this by trying it both ways. I identified my own best learning mode through trial and error. Yours is different from mine. What is it?

Academicians and theoreticians can tell you a lot about how people learn, and if you are interested in the study of learning, then by all means look into it. But what it comes down to is purely a matter of you figuring how you learn, and the only way to do that is to try things and then honestly look at the results.

In addition to reading, I love learning by interacting with other people, so pair programming is a wonderful practice for me, not just because it produces better code, but because I learn a lot.

Think about how you learned the things you know best

How did you learn, for example, to judge whether a design is good or bad? If you're a cowboy, your answer might be, "Shucks, pardner, I just code it right up and if it works, then I call the design good!"

Well, that's not going to be enough today. You need to have a process in place that allows you to explore alternative ideas before you spend time coding.

I need pictures when I talk about design; words are not sufficient. Without pictures, I find I don't learn what the design really is. It took me a long time to realize that this was true for me. I built one of the first graphical modeling tools without doing any modeling—because I didn't know any better. Ironic, isn't it?

Then I got a job somewhere else using this same modeling tool to talk about a design. The company that hired me wanted to thoroughly explore the design problem we were facing, and we used the tool to do it.

The light bulb went on for me: I realized the massive number of powerful ways you could talk about a problem by using some sort of graphical language. I gained the ability to look at things in a different way, and to communicate about them with different people.

So take some time, reflect on yourself, look for the things that help you learn better, and then do more of them. You can afford that time, because writing code today isn't very time consuming compared to how it used to be. If you can keep your knowledge base growing ahead of others in your field, you'll keep doing better and better.

The big picture is the small picture is the big picture

"What am I interested in?"

That is the really important question.

Conscious software development involves keeping up with yourself, keeping up with technology, and keeping up with your team. It involves showing up and being available to all the people and activities that are around you. So when I talk about "learning" in the context of software development, I'm not talking about technical skills alone; I mean learning what's going on all around you now, and learning to see and embrace what is coming.

One of my earliest programming jobs was in Australia in the 1960s, working for a large research organization. Their culture held that everyone in the company should spend at least four hours a week learning new things.

They didn't want us to focus on the incremental, learning how to do something new with the technologies we already knew and used; they wanted us to look further afield. So we spent that time learning and then we gave reports about what we had learned.

Learning isn't just about getting better at the skills and tools you are currently using. It's not just about things like: How do I become a better Java programmer? It's important that you don't spend all of your time down in the weeds, because if you do you will have a hard time seeing the big things that are coming at you—and big things come at you all the time.

The small stuff is best learnt by doing. Doing the actual coding work and talking to other developers about it, that is how I learn the smaller, lower level stuff that I need to be very good at—but I also need to be very good at the high level view, and a lot of the reading I do is about the big picture.

You need to learn to move quickly back and forth between the details and the big picture—you should always be moving, oscillating between those things.

I try to keep my learning around the big picture stuff less programmatic. I do that by following what's interesting to me. There is so much information around us now that it is easy to get lost, and it is easy to feel like you are wasting a lot of time wandering around amongst the seemingly random stuff that is out there floating in the ether, simply because there is so much of it.

But it is important to get lost!

It is important that you do some wandering. This is the reason consciousness is such a difficult discipline to master—you might need to get lost now in order to see clearly later on. This requires you to trust both yourself and the universe around you a great deal. But if mendicant monks can do it, you can, too!

Why is it so important to keep an eye on the big picture?

One of the characteristics of the art of software development is that the better a developer you are, the higher the level of abstraction at which you work.

That doesn't mean you can't be focused and very good in some specific area, but for me it has never been sufficient to be an expert in how to do something. I was a world-class expert in Smalltalk when I was working in that language, no doubt about it. And I was interested in other things at the same time.

When Smalltalk faded out of fashion the bigger picture I had constructed, my larger view, contributed to the principles and practices we now know as agile software development. Each step of my career has been incubated in the earlier steps.

When agile concepts were first coming together, all those higher level views and patterns made sense to me because, while I knew pattern implementation in Smalltalk, I'd been studying and thinking about things at that higher level of abstraction as well.

If you really want to be conscious about what you are doing and conscious about where things are going, about the larger picture, then you will spend a noticeable amount of time learning.

The value of seeing the larger picture is that even when you're up to your eyebrows in code on a project, you'll find yourself capable of the big *Aha!* moment. Suddenly you'll discover, "Wait a minute, I've been doing things I'm really good at, but if I do things this other way I can get three times as much done! I can get five times as much done!"

Getting down into the detail, and getting better at those details down in the code, will give you tens of percentage points of improvement. But is that really good enough? What if we are looking for hundreds of percentage points of improvement? Because at the end of the day, we really want to get much better at what we are doing, not just a little better at what we are doing. The tens do add up, but the hundreds are the result of real breakthroughs.

How do we think about something differently?

Can we take something that someone else discovered in another discipline and apply that to what we are doing, so that now whole sets of problems completely go away? That kind of exponential change and improvement is what we are talking about when we talk about learning.

To get there, you have to have enough of a view outside your little focal area, you have to be able to see those larger patterns when they are there, and to apply them.

I remember when I learned geometry in high school. I was taught the theorems like everyone else. I could solve problems by applying the "best" theorem by rote as it were. It was boring to me. And tedious.

I was also taught the principles and the abstractions. With these in hand I could solve the problems I was given by applying the principles and abstractions. It was harder in some way but very challenging: How can I go back to fundamental abstractions? This learning has served me well in software.

Later in college and after I would go back and look at physics problems and grab some interesting physics problem and solve it with basic geometry, just to see how those things worked together, tying the ends off, exercising those muscles by reaching for higher levels of abstraction in domains that I did not necessarily know so much about.

I had the pleasure of attending lectures by Richard Feynman at Caltech where I was able to hone some of these skills. For a deep example of what I mean you may wish to visit *Feynman's Lost Lecture* published by Norton. In that he uses the most basic concepts of geometry and physics to show why planets circle the sun in ellipses. I certainly never have achieved his skill but the direction is clear.

In software the use of patterns is a very clear example of useful abstraction. Understanding the forces and constraints involved yields well known solutions.

Deep concepts and abstracts show up for me as a software developer all the time, and I consider learning at this level incredibly important to being a conscious software developer.

On Time

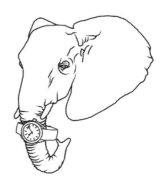

Once upon a time, early in my career, I found myself the primary developer on a project to build a tool to test software. I spent a lot of time revisiting my own code, creating new versions, improving the performance, refactoring, that kind of thing.

At one point, I found myself stumped by a particularly sticky problem. As I looked through all of the various versions, I noticed that I had been oscillating between two different approaches to solving the problem. I'd solve it one way, and we'd put it out there, and then we'd find out that solution didn't work so well, so then I'd go back to the old way—when I looked at what I'd done, I found I had gone back and forth at least three times.

What that said to me was that the design was not really working. It turned out that I needed a bridge pattern, but I didn't realize this until I finally noticed how the software had gone back and forth over time. Eventually I did get there, with the help of these observations.

The point is that I found it truly useful to look back at how my software had changed over time, and even more useful, moving forward, to think ahead about how it might change over time even as I wrote it.

Knowing software is going to change over time is a basic assumption, but we often act, when we're writing it, as though it's not going to change. We just write it and skip merrily off to do something else. But in the commercial world, software gets revisited a lot as we improve it and move from version 1.0 to version 2.0 to version 2.1 and so on.

Software lives in time

There's a reason we "write" code, but "develop" software. Code may be written one line at a time, but all successful software lives its life over a period of time.

By this I mean that, yes, while a few companies have made their mark with version 1.0, it is rare that any company makes a lot of money on version 1.0. The value of software is almost always created when we hold our noses, roll up our sleeves, and go back into the code, over and over again.

Most of us have the opportunity to observe our software over time, quite often at the team level, but even at the individual level. We write it, then we go back to visit it later. We add to it, or change it in some way, we keep after it—software is not something we do once and never look at again. And of course, it may not even be you looking at your software over time—or maybe you're spending your time up to your elbows in software someone else wrote.

What do I mean when I say that software changes over time? What changes?

We change methods, we change their names, we add to objects, we make new objects, we put things together and break things apart.

Taking a moment to look at that process is useful because you can learn more about the quality of your software by looking at how it has changed than by looking at any kind of plan—past, present or future.

You can't understand how your code works—or doesn't work—without first observing how it behaves, and behavior shows itself over time. But you also can't expect to fully understand what you're observing until you know enough about yourself to see how your own internal processes, your assumptions and habits, affect how you interact with the design and how these too may change.

In the project I described earlier, I eventually observed that our design wasn't quite good enough, because it kept allowing me to oscillate between two alternatives, both of which were less effective than they could have been.

One of the characteristics of good design is that good design stays relatively intact over time, through any number of changes. You don't really know that a design is good, that the design is appropriate for solving the problem, until you observe—over time—that the changes you make don't dramatically affect the design.

How fast or slow do you like to go?

Do you write a lot of code and throw it out quickly? That's a fine thing! It may be better for you to throw together code that works and get your tests working, and then go back to clean it all up. If that's your style—and I find it to be a style that works for me personally—then it's very important you do that clean up. If you don't clean up after yourself, you will be left with dead-ends in place.

When it comes to styles of working, I am a type known as a quick starter. I like to get started! If that's your style, then how is that reflected in your code? Do you bang it out with a lot of debt? I do.

When I write software from scratch, I write it with some design debt, knowing that I will need to go back and pay that debt down before too much time passes. If I wait too long, I find that it's much harder for me to go back in and look at the code, because it's a mess. It's also much harder for other people to look at my code!

You might want to inquire into how you do your development in time. Do you do use case development? Do you tend to do it in layers, drilling down, or do you take a deep breath and dive deep first? I think that a deep dive through the entire application is a better way to do it. Some people call that "the happy path" because it feels so good to do development that way. Of course, you go through and clean stuff up after you surface...right?

Or do you tend to get hung up on all the details of every little thing you encounter along the way—a not-so-happy path?

In agile development, we find that taking the happy path first often works best. It may not always be appropriate or even possible, but in general that's a better way to write software, so you need to know if that's how you are working, and if that's not how you work, then you might need to learn a new way of working.

Look back to move forward

I knew I had reached a certain level of maturity in my design process when I discovered that I had written code that hadn't changed in seven years. I knew this only because I had been keeping track of the code I wrote for over twelve years. To me that is a mark of a good design: it's doing what it does, and it's doing it well. I'm not adding stuff to it, because when I have an object that does one thing, I let it do that thing, and when I need new things I make new objects to do those new things. That kind of encapsulation is a quality of good design, and I noticed that my code was becoming more stable over time. To see this, I had to look at it over time.

So as I got better at writing new, resilient code and had to change old code less, I also noticed that I didn't have to write so many new tests, and this in turn made my designs and my code even more resilient.

If you are not conscious about how you write software, if you are not conscious about your own work patterns, then it's hard to know how to improve your code—and how to improve your patterns.

So look hard, sit down with someone else and look at your code, even if you don't have a formal code review process in your organization. Get some perspective on your code from someone else's point of view, and look specifically at how the code has changed over the lifespan of the software itself.

All code changes. Knowing that it does change over time and being conscious of that change starts with you, individually, learning about your style, what you do, where you are comfortable and where you could improve.

Software is a Team Sport

I view software development as a team sport. Until agile development methods came along, I had never talked about it in those terms, but I'd been playing it that way for a long time.

I've referred to consciousness as finding out what is happening inside of the individual. But how does introspection relate to playing on a team?

I think back to when I followed the San Francisco 49ers, and there were two people on that team, Joe Montana who was a quarterback, and Jerry Rice, who was a receiver. They were quite a pair!

These two men, these two players, were very different, and each of them was an excellent player in his own right, and yet for both, the team always came first. That was the dynamic.

Now, it is true that the team can't be as good as it can be if you are not being as good as you can be individually. That means your individual practice matters; the things you do individually matter greatly.

A lot of people who advocate agile methods sell the individual short, implying that we don't want individual contributors to stand out.

That's not true at all—what is true is that we want people who are very conscious in their work.

How does this kind of consciousness manifest itself? In my experience, it mostly shows up in the communication that goes on within a team, because great teams are all about communication. Jerry Rice and Joe Montana practiced together so much that Joe always knew what Jerry was going to do, and Jerry knew what Joe was going to do.

They didn't have to sit down and talk about it and make decisions, they just knew. So it looked like magic when it happened, because they seemed to always know what to do.

In the long run, it all comes down to something that's really simple and yet really difficult, and that is that you as an individual need to hold up your end of the communication.

All communication, even in a group, occurs between two people, each of whom has to hold up his or her end. When both people do, you achieve something I like to call congruence. Other people call it different things—some call it being authentic. In the men's movement you hear a lot about being an "authentic male." I prefer the term congruent because it conveys this idea that I need to be and act from where I am.

For instance, let's say that you and I are having a disagreement, and we are trying to come to some understanding. It doesn't help if I throw up my hands and say, "Whatever!" when I don't really agree. When I say that I agree even when I don't, that's incongruent— that's me not being true to what's going on within myself. That's not high-performance communication.

The communication that we want is the kind where everyone is being as clear as they can about where they are.

Now, this isn't a license to act out. If you are mad, being authentic or congruent doesn't mean you start throwing things around. But it might mean just saying, "I'm feeling mad right now." It might only mean recognizing that you are mad inside yourself, knowing what is going on inside you.

When I first learned about congruence and about ways of being that aren't congruent, I wasn't very good at it, I can assure you. I had to learn to do it well.

The psychologist Virginia Satir describes several of what she calls "communication stances," and I find many of those are common on software teams.

There's the *blaming stance*, when you're standing above someone, literally or figuratively, and looking down your finger. You can see and feel your body doing it, looking down with a scowl on your face.

There's the *placating stance*: hands up, fending off: Oh! Please! I didn't mean to! I used to do that with my bosses all the time, whenever something wouldn't go quite right. It's hard to admit right now, at this moment in time, but it's true. That's what I tend to do: I placate.

When you assume a *hyper-rational stance*, you go completely up into your head and lose track of what's going on with the rest of your body. You are seething inside, so you get super rational. We see a lot of that in our business. Lots of judgment.

Another stance I see a lot of and one that isn't on Satir's list, is *indifference*. "It doesn't matter." The big "whatever." People tend to turn away when they express indifference.

I can see myself doing those things. I can look at what my body is doing, and I can think about what I want to do with my body, or maybe what I wanted to do but stopped myself from doing. These assumed stances are all just ways to keep ourselves from being where we are at, authentically. The subtlety is that it is not so much about changing how you act, but about being mindful of what's going on with you.

Jim McCarthy wrote a book called *Software For Your Head*, in which he talked about a practice that he used on scrum teams for the daily stand up, that daily meeting where people on a team check in with one another about what's going on. In addition to reporting out on what they did since the last stand up, what they planned to do before the next, and what impediments they faced, each team member would give a one or two word description of their emotional state that day. They would say things like, "I'm mad," or "I'm feeling joyful," or "I'm feeling cool today, a little depressed."

The purpose of the statement was to help introduce some team-level awareness of what was going on with people. If someone on your team is comfortable letting the rest of you know, "I had a fight with my sweetheart this morning, so I'm kind of mad," then you have the opportunity to decide that maybe today is not a good time to ask that person to make a very sensitive architectural decision. You'll know that if you do make that decision today, it may not work out quite so well, so it may be better to wait a little bit, to be patient.

This isn't about acting out, or even about expressing everything you are feeling all the time. It's about recognizing where you are and claiming where you are emotionally, even if it's silently and just for yourself. This will let you have more authentic conversations, and in turn you will feel better, and be more authentic. It will also be easier for you to change your emotional state, if you find you want to, because you will no longer be holding a rigid stance.

This activity of learning to be more congruent, more authentic, is difficult. It takes time and introspection. Be patient with yourself as you explore this area.

To play a team sport well, we cannot be rigid—we have got to be able to move. When Jerry and Joe were playing for the 49ers neither one of them ever stood still. They had to know what was going on, inside and out, and to move accordingly.

On reflection

If you practice agile development using methods like scrum, then one of the recommendations is that you regularly hold something called a retrospective. A retrospective is about taking some time to stand together as a team, looking and thinking about the dynamics of your team's process with an eye to improving it. And a great deal of the issues that surface will revolve around communication.

Even in a group setting, communication is often a two way street— not a six way intersection. There are usually two people directly engaging at any given time. That means that in a retrospective, when discussions are going on, most of the time you are not in the midst of directly participating in one of those interactions. This gives you an opportunity to sit back and look at what is happening at the team level.

In scrum we recommend that retrospectives last an hour and a half, and for newer teams maybe a little longer. Team members need sufficient time to disengage from the usual hustle and bustle.

We also recommend to have some food on the table, because food is where we humans spend more time socially interacting. Family meals, dining out with friends, dating—those are all times when we practice our richest social interactions, and that's the level at which we want our interactions during the retrospective to take place.

Retrospectives are a wonderful time for you to practice being present, being there with the team and observing. And when you do comment, the subtleness of the group dynamic is such that it's not about you chiming in and saying what's going on *over there* in someone else; it's about you saying what's going on *in here*, in you.

This is a subtle difference. You do want to communicate what you're seeing in the group, but you want to communicate it from the point of view of what's going on within *you*.

This is the paradox of how team interactions work: that the interaction that is going on *over there* is best understood by you talking about what's going on *inside you*, or by me talking about what's going on *inside me*. This makes no sense! It makes no sense whatsoever that this is the way to move things forward! But it is. The kind of communication we see in very high performing teams is an information flow that is just going on all the time

I've seen teams that have been together for ten years that now barely talk about issues and problems. Things like tasking and planning happen so quickly you barely notice them going by, because everybody knows what to do. A few words pass between them, and then they scribble something down and make little cards—all that team needs are two or three words to a card, because everybody already knows what the shorthand means. You don't have to write a spec. These people understand not just what they're talking about, but how they're talking about it. If they do have an issue, they jump straight to talking about the communication issue, rather than dwelling on the problem itself. They know the real question is always: *What about the context isn't clear?*

When I see two people really going at it in a discussion, the first thing I think is, wait a minute, do we have a shared understanding of the context? What happens in those situations is we forget that the mind is not the tool that we should be using. This is the part that's so hard to grasp, especially for those of us who got into computers because interacting with other humans was very scary. We thought it would be better to interact with computers, but it turns out that we have to interact with humans anyway and—even harder to admit—we actually like it. Admitting we like to communicate may be a separate problem, but we actually do like it.

The level of communication we see going on in high-performing teams comes out of the heart. It is about the connectivity that we have with each other as human beings. Not the heart that brings flowers and says, "I love you and I want to be with you forever," but the place in the heart where we feel what's going on with each other rather than merely thinking it. The place where we have compassion for what's going on inside one another.

Now, compassion is a loaded term for a lot of people, but what compassion means for me is really just the ability to feel what other people are going through. So, if I'm talking about a tough issue that has confused someone I'm talking to, compassion comes into it when I acknowledge all the times that I'm confused myself, and even if I don't share their confusion of the moment, I can empathize with them because I know it sometimes happens to me, too.

A bridge is built between us when that occurs, and I can't build that bridge when I talk about an issue from my mind. My head may not even understand the other person's words, yet when I bring compassion to the conversation, there is a richness of communication that occurs, and less need for the mind to understand it.

When it comes down to it, we work with each other in order to achieve that sense of connection, for that sense of working on something we all love, working on a product we all want to be proud of. We want to be part of a team that gets something done. None of those things is about the mind. Those are about the heart, the feelings we have about each other and about the work we do. It's wonderful when this occurs, because when it does, I can go home and take that feeling of fullness, that feeling of being involved, along with me. I take that home to my family and then it's there with them too. My family is moved by what moves me at work, because that richness I've brought into my life gives me more in that part of my life as well. And when my family life is going well, then I can bring that to my work environment as a support as well.

This is a topic which many people in our industry don't want to talk about, but it's present and it's true, and I think we do need to talk about it. I see too many people who hate what they are doing, who literally cannot stand to come to work. I understand why they might have to knuckle down and do a job they hate, but to me that is incredibly painful.

Can I relate to that situation? Can I relate to them? Can I feel my way back to the times that I've had to do that? Yes, and it was painful.

I can recall the times when I have not liked what I was doing, and that recollection lets me be there with that person. It's not about getting them to talk about how they feel—I'm not talking about that. I'm talking about me being there and feeling that pain that I have felt in my own life at various times, and recalling the compassion I have for myself when that occurs; accepting those parts of me that operate like that.

Perhaps you can feel a little bit more, and this will let you be with and express yourself to the other people around you.

Communication

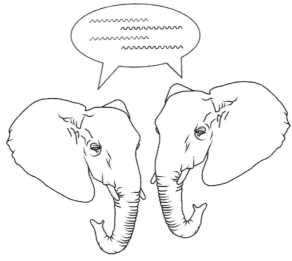

As software developers, we live and work in an environment so complex that no one of us can "solve the whole problem" by ourselves. The mythological days of the single person writing the application that takes the world by storm are definitely over—if they ever really existed. We build software in teams today, so there is a whole lotta communication going on all around us, all the time.

However many people you may have in your work group, it helps to remember that interactions between people are always one on one—there are always two people, even when there are three people!

What I mean is that there is always a communicator and a listener. An advantage to having a work group of three people in the room is that at any given moment, while two people are talking and interacting about some topic, the third is watching and listening.

Now, this third person, this observer, may have something they want to add to the discussion, but then that usually turns into another conversation between that person and one of the other two.

Having three people in a conversation, in the roles of communicator, listener and observer, adds an interesting dynamic when you're working on a problem, and in my opinion three is much better than two for this very reason. But right now, let's dig into this problem of just two people who are having some sort of interaction.

Most of us think of this thing called communication as unfolding roughly like this: you say something, I hear it, I figure out what it means, and then I respond. It is a simple formula:

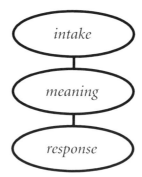

Now, all of that is true, but there is a lot more going on, and if you are going to be fully conscious, you will need to employ a richer communication model than this basic, three-step one.

One model that I have used successfully is psychologist Virginia Satir's "ingredients of an interaction." Satir's model adds some key steps to the foregoing model, like this:

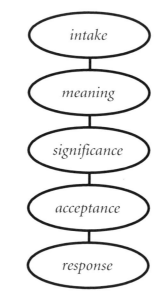

The first thing that happens is *intake*: you say something, and I take it in. Perhaps you say to me, "Hey, Jeff, what are you doing for lunch?"

The question to me then is, "What did that person just say?" What were the real words? What was the body language, the physicality of it? What things just happened that I heard and saw? Often when we hear someone begin talking, we immediately start trying to figure out how to respond, or why they are wrong, and we literally cannot hear what they say. So the first step is to focus on intake, on really hearing what the person communicating has said.

I might get so hungry when I hear the word "lunch," for example, that I fail to parse the rest of your question. Or maybe the question caused me to remember suddenly that I am late to meet someone else for lunch! It is possible, as you can see, to have a lot of reactions to someone's act of speech that have nothing to do with really listening to them.

The next step is to figure out what is the *meaning*. As a listener, I am hearing what was said in a context, and that context helps determine the meaning. If someone asks me a question in one context, the answer may be completely different than the answer to the same question in another context.

If I am sitting next to you in our team's work room, I may interpret your question, "What are you doing for lunch?" as an invitation. If, on the other hand, you ask me the question while I'm walking out the door, I'll assume you are merely asking me where I'm headed.

The same words, the same intake, can have different meanings based on the context you are in. We assume that we all "get" those meanings and we do that based on our interactions. If we had to explain everything in great detail all the time, then communication would be very slow indeed! So context provides the container for the conversation.

But then the next steps are more nuanced. Rather than just responding, there are a couple of other things happening. The first one is that I ascribe some *significance* to what you said. When you ask me to have lunch with you, the significance might be greater than what the mere words convey. Maybe I've been looking forward to spending time with you, and this question provides me with an opportunity to do so. Or maybe I think you want to talk to me about the broken build, and I take the fact that it warrants a lunch to mean it's going to be a very serious conversation indeed. Or maybe you are a poor lunch companion who talks nonstop about your stamp collection--with your mouth full. Or maybe you and I are friends and have been wanting to try that new Peruvian place down the street, and lunch means merely... lunch. That layer of significance will inform my answer.

The overt meaning of your words were that you want to have a meal with me, but the significance to me may be that I feel anything from eagerness, to fear, to disappointment, to hunger.

Which brings us to the next part of the communication equation: *acceptance*. How do I feel about the impending lunchtime conversation with you? Maybe I'm excited. Or maybe I didn't really want to have the conversation, so I'm apprehensive. I need to check how I feel, and accept my internal reactions. Then and only then, depending on how I feel, I will *respond*.

So again, the steps are: *intake, meaning, significance, acceptance* and *response*.

The last four of those are actually based more on what's going on inside of me as a listener, far more than they are based on what's going on with you as the communicator. The closer I get to accurately perceiving what's going on within myself, the more my past will affect what is going on in the present. If I have been trying for the past three weeks to get time to have a conversation with you, then my response may be one of eagerness. I might say, "Let's grab a bite together!" while if I just don't like your company I may say, "Sorry, Bob, I just ate."

Either way, I am not really responding to what you said, am I? I'm responding to what's inside of me, and to our personal history together.

Now if you're in any sort of relationship, especially a spousal relationship, this sort of thing happens all the time. Because we spend so much time with each other we have all this shared history, and it colors our responses, what meaning we ascribe to what was said, how significant we think it is. "She asked me to take the garbage out again! She must think I never take the garbage out!" All those things that happened to us lead to all these extra layers of meaning that we put on things.

And in a work context especially, we are likely to have unwritten rules about how we express ourselves, or even about what is acceptable to express. "I'm not allowed to show them my displeasure," you may feel, or, "I'm not allowed to talk about the fact that I'm really disappointed in this person." Maybe we're working on a project together, and I feel I'm not allowed to challenge your design, even though I don't like the design, or there may be politics! One wins and one loses.

There are many ways to go about becoming more conscious of what we are doing on our end of the conversation. Because you can imagine that if all these subtexts are present all the time, and we are each responding out of our own interior responses, that very quickly our conversation can cease to have anything to do with the real topic at hand.

A great deal of the work involved in exploring consciousness is about getting in touch with those things that are going on within us below the level of conscious awareness, and bringing that rich material to the fore. There is a lot of data now showing that a great many of these patterns governing how we interact are set when we are fairly young, so a great deal of the work is about going back and exploring how you learned to be the way you are.

You can start out fairly simply, just by looking at these five steps instead of just three. When you are having trouble with conversations or interactions with people, then you can start slowing the process down and teasing apart that question of, "What's really going on with me? Am I reacting to what that person is saying now, or reacting to our history?"

A lot of this is about learning how to interact in the present instead of in the past. The good news is that it is fun to explore this stuff, and you will find that communication is one of those things that can get a lot better very quickly.

Mental Models

How do you think about software when you are developing it? How do you think when you're in self-development mode? I'm talking specifically about how *you* think, because all of us are a little different.

Some people are more visual, some are more textual, and these different people have different ways of conceptualizing their work. When I started out in software development, everything was written in assembly language, and I did quite a bit of operating system development. It worked like this: there would be some sort of stimulus, an event, a request coming from outside the system that would precipitate this flow of things that would occur inside the system.

That was the essence of procedural programming—events occurred and procedures would be called up by the events. The mechanism of routines, call-and-response procedures, were built into the languages I was using.

That was how I thought about software for quite a long time. But as I learned more and became a better developer, I found myself wanting to understand how things worked at higher levels of abstraction.

I worked in satellite tracking, so I knew about the levels of and the kinds of calculations that had to occur, and had learned about errors in propagation, loss of accuracy, and all those issues around analytics and calculations. But I had been in software development for 15 years before I moved into objects, at a time when the object metaphor was coming on strong.

For me, objects turned out to be a very powerful way to think about problems, and to encapsulate solutions. When I started thinking about the world in terms of objects, I found life much easier. I started drawing diagrams and thinking visually. Now, I had done that before with flow charts, when we were doing procedural work, just because I had always found thinking visually to be much more useful for me when looking at the larger picture. If I only looked at the code, I found it far too easy to get lost in the details of the procedures.

I also found that I had difficulty communicating with people when I only talked about the code, because everybody looks at code a little differently, and I think it is important that we communicate with each other about the software we are writing, and what we understand about it. This is why I like modeling languages, especially graphical modeling languages. The most common is UML (Unified Modeling Language). But whatever language you use, the important thing is for your team to have a common way to talk about code, and I have found that communicating textually or verbally is just not enough. In the same way that the Agile Manifesto suggested that we should have working software and not just documents that talk about the software, I think there is also a change that occurs if you use visual techniques rather than just textual techniques to talk about software. But remember that not everyone responds and learns visually, so you need to find way of communicating, your team's best way of communicating.

Me, I find that I can see objects in space—I just literally see them in space. And because I have done enough modeling, when I think about problems I'm always constructing in my mind a mental model whether or not I am actually making one using UML. So when I work on a software project, whether at the highest level, or down deep in the code, I am forever updating the model inside my head.

As we know, a model is always just a representation of reality; reality is not the model, and the reality needs to drive the model, not the other way around, so I want that model to stay as close to the code as possible. Since I have worked with systems like Smalltalk and Scala and other functional languages, which require yet another model, I recognize that each language or system requires that you do things differently, and may require you to model objects differently—I have learned that I shouldn't mix these models up.

The reason for this is that different models have different strengths and different weaknesses. Object oriented models have a tendency to be a little static and this doesn't make it as easy to think about the dynamics. For a lot of the early object oriented work, we considered this good enough—having objects that encapsulated stuff so that one knew it was contained was just better than procedural programming in terms of understanding your systems. The way I think about it now, with the benefit of many years' hindsight, is that objects' main claim to fame is that they make it much easier to maintain your system.

That is very useful, but objects do present other problems, in that they can make it hard to understand the flow and the bird's eye view of what's going on. So, because it is hard to do that with objects, and because I like to think of software in that way, this creates a weakness in how I think about things, and I need to be aware of that.

Every modeling technique has strengths and weakness like this, so if you use a modeling technique to such an extent that is dominant in how you think, you need to know its weaknesses, because they will be your own weaknesses.

None of this is to say that having weaknesses can be avoided, or is even a problem!

Maybe you develop a set of questions you need to ask yourself, rigorously, to make sure you're not cultivating blind spots:

How do I see the big picture?

Is there some technique I can use?

Can I do something that makes it easier for me to understand the big picture flow?

Or maybe you need to pair up with someone else who is not weak in that same area. The two of you together will have some synergy, and the combination will be stronger than either one of you by yourselves. I like abstractions, for instance. Abstractions make it very easy for me to think about things. Some people have a lot of trouble with abstractions, though, so maybe they need to work with someone like me who does get them.

This kind of helping is not just about compensating for weaknesses and sharing strengths, but about learning how to do things better. It's not conceptually difficult to do abstraction, flow, encapsulation, all of those things that as humans we do pretty naturally, but we all have different levels of experience in these, and different levels of expertise, and can learn from one another.

Do some experiments. Find out what works for you, and what works for the people around you. When you talk about things, can they understand you? Explore how you think and how you operate, because knowing that will make you very much more effective as you continue on in the software development profession.

Your Body (Yes, you have one!)

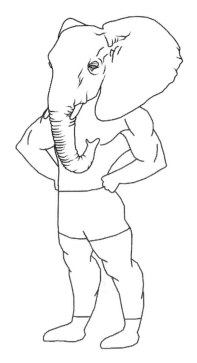

Now I want to talk about something very bizarre in the context of software development—your body. Specifically, I want to talk about how your body is involved in the work that you do as a software developer.

A lot of us don't pay attention to our bodies when we sit down in front of a computer. In fact for many of us, the body just mysteriously melts away when we are fully engaged in our work.

When my wife and I first got together over 30 years ago, she learned pretty quickly that she couldn't get my attention by talking to me when I was at the computer, because I was just gone.

"It's like you're *inside* the computer," she said.

Sometimes she laughed at this, and sometimes she didn't, but eventually we came to an agreement: when she needed my attention she would tap me on the shoulder, then allow me thirty seconds to gather myself together, come back into my body, and respond.

I did some mountain climbing in my youth, and when you do
something like mountain climbing, it is very important that you stay
in touch with your body and stay focused on what is going on around
you, because if you don't you can fall off the mountain, which isn't
healthy.

We don't have to worry about such things happening to our bodies
when we are sitting in front of a computer—and yet the body is
there!

So if it is there, what is its utility—what is this body there for? Why
don't we have to pay attention? Or do we?

Usually when my wife wanted to pull me out of the computer, it was
to ask a question or get my help to solve a problem. Sometimes it
was to get me to eat something, because I would disappear into the
computer and wouldn't eat for hours on end, and then I'd emerge all
grumpy and crabby due to the simple fact that I hadn't eaten.

If you are a programmer, these are doubtless things you've
experienced and laughed about yourself—and it is true that it is great
fun to get lost ghosting around inside of a machine—but there is
something else going on when that happens, something that I learned
about only in the last decade or so.

What I learned is that we software developers are physical beings. We
are animals. Our bodies have a role in our lives, and that role isn't just
to hold the brain stem up.

The body has deep knowledge about what is going on inside of itself
but also, believe it or not, of what is going on inside the computer.

I have discovered that if I'm stuck, having trouble solving a
complicated problem, my body can usually help. If I change my body,
change what it's doing, then it can help get me unstuck.

We've all heard stories or had experiences of this: you get up and
go take a shower, and only then do you get an idea that changes

everything. You got away from it, you changed the space a little bit physically, and that helped free you up mentally.

If you haven't experienced that phenomenon, you may want to pay attention and notice your physical circumstances, what's going on when that hard-won solution finally drops. Chances are you've done something different, made some change in your mind's environment to allow that to happen.

When you are feeling stuck, get up and go do something else. Stand up at least every hour or so and wander around a little bit, shake your body up. That will help you maintain your physical well-being, but it also helps the mind. This may seem obvious, but there is something subtler that also occurs when you ask your body for help solving the problems you are facing in your mind.

Years ago when I worked with Ward Cunningham we used our bodies in design work, using a technique call CRC cards. Each card represented a class (or object) in the system and we would explore the interactions of the classes (or objects) by physically acting out the flow of control/information. Each person would take a card or two and then talk out the passing of control from person to person. Note-taking on the cards captured any new insights. Our bodies made it much easier to understand what was going on as well as what might need to go on.

Here is another, more subtle approach: If I've been noodling around on a design problem and can't figure out which way to go, I might get up, walk around, do all that. But I might also take it a step further and actually ask my body help me.

Let's say there are two ways I can think of to accomplish something, and I'm trying to figure out which might be the best way. In order to enlist my body's help in making that decision, I might logically or even physically represent those two things in different spaces—I might draw a little sketch of each, and put one over here, and the other over there, across the room. Then I take a seat somewhere between them and think for a bit, waiting to see which one my body wants to go toward. It won't be equal. The decision—my instinctual, unarticulated inclination toward which solution I know in my bones to be best—will show up in subtle gestures and movement.

This is not an easy trick to get the hang of, and it takes some quietness to make it happen. I'm not talking about the quietness of an empty room, but a quietness within yourself. You have to be willing to silence your mind—or at the very least disciplined enough to not listen to it—because your mind may well be sitting there saying, "Blah! Blah! Blah!," trying its level best to "help" you decide one way or the other. Unchecked, your mind will likely keep trying out lots of possibilities—maybe you do this, which means that, and what about making a checklist? All that stuff. Our minds are constantly sifting through all that conscious, rational stuff. But for me, if I get my body to move on it like a Ouija board, I'll go one way or another, and most times, this works out extremely well! I arrive at a better decision by listening to my body than I would if I had listened to just my mind.

This is how I disengage my mind from the tyranny of the "what if's" and get back to having fun, and I find it has saved me not just time, but a lot of worry.

On Architecture

Architecture is an interesting word in the software arena. We talk about architecture all the time, and it's this big thing that's supposed to happen with great fanfare at the beginning of a project—and then we are supposed to stick it away in a box and forget all about it while we get on with the design and coding.

I don't think that works very well at all. I think about architecture in a different way.

First, a detour. Take a look at the architecture of a car: a car's "architecture" consists of four wheels, a chassis, a steering wheel, at least two seats, an ignition system, an engine. Cup holders? Maybe so—sure, cup holders!

Taken together those architectural components spell out "car" to our brain. And our brains make use of this architectural big picture all the time—when we slide behind the wheel, we assume knowledge that all these architectural elements are there, even though we don't think about them explicitly.

That's what we'd like to do with our software architecture. We'd like to use it while we build software, much the way we use the car's architecture to drive to the 7-Eleven for a carton of milk.

The architecture of your car is not invisible, it's just something you stop noticing all the time because you've come to rely on it. You don't want to stop thinking about the architecture because it's time to move on to the next phase of what you're doing; you want to know the architecture so well that you don't have to think about it.

But what exactly is architecture, really? In software, what does the term architecture actually mean?

I like to use an old-fashioned definition of architecture here, which says simply that:

> *Architecture is the way we think about things so that when new things occur we know where to put them.*

If a new object shows up in our domain, then we know where in the architecture that object should be placed, or how it should be partitioned between the pieces of the implementation architecture. In that sense, architecture is nothing less than a framework within which to speak and think. It is the idealization of the structure of the project.

In software development, we encounter a couple of different kinds of architecture: domain architecture and implementation architecture.

Domain architecture

Domain architecture addresses the question: How do we think about the application?

In extreme programming, the term "system metaphor" describes the domain architecture, and it's just what it sounds like: a way of describing the system we're building by comparing it to another system we already know a lot about. This shorthand helps us visualize what we're up to. Ron Jeffries describes a system metaphor as "a simple evocative description of how the program works, such as 'this program works like a hive of bees, going out for pollen and bringing it back to the hive' as a description for an agent-based information retrieval system."

In practice, it isn't enough to think about the domain model, or domain architecture, as being about the application; it is really about how we think about the problem the application will solve. What are the major ways we talk about it? What are the major constructions that we use to talk about it? And when a new problem shows up we have to say to ourselves, does this fit with our current set of constructs? Do the constructs we have now for the domain fit? Or do we need new ones?

Too often we forget to say, "Let's take a fresh look at the problem." Instead we say, "Oh, here is a new element, a new construction that we never thought about before, let's make it work" and we try to put it on top of something that's already there. This is how a faulty sense of what the domain architecture is can create very poor systems coupled in unintentional ways.

Now, this may sound to you like I am talking about design, not architecture, and in some ways I am, because architecture to me is the big pieces—the big chunks of design that we decide on early and that become expensive to change over time.

Implementation architecture

To many people, the term architecture often means implementation architecture. Are we client-server based? Are we browser-based with a server? Are we using SOA? These are all thought of as architectures, but to me these are implementation architectures.

I want to separate out the implementation architecture from the domain architecture, and from how we think about the domain. It's very important that we make that separation, because we naturally tend to make decisions that are driven or contained or controlled by our implementation architecture. And if that implementation architecture is not suitable to solving the problem, then we have a more serious problem that we don't even see. We want to be conscious about it, to see what's really going on when we make those decisions, so we can separate the elements out and get at the right questions to ask in the first place.

Recently I was working on a project where we were seriously constrained by the implementation architecture. We had to bastardize the domain so badly that when we were done the domain didn't look very much like the original problem anymore. And since the domain now didn't address the problem, reaching a solution started to become very difficult.

This is why we need to pay attention to these two different ways of thinking about architecture: the domain side of the architecture and the implementation side of the architecture. They inform each other, and they can help each other. Choosing the right implementation architecture can make a big difference in how easily you can implement the domain, so you want to make these decisions consciously. Keep asking yourself: What are the trade-offs?

Implementation architecture is a lot about performance and scalability, and how you put those things together, and it even encompasses the larger view of user experience. Domain architecture is about the problem, and solving the problem. Those two are not the same thing, and people who try to make them the same thing never quite get the domain to work. This is because the implementation architecture is stronger than the domain. It overpowers the domain, even when it shouldn't, because it is easier to change the domain to fit the architecture than to change the architecture to fit the domain. Alas, the result will always be less than optimal solutions to our problems.

A comment on Domain Driven Design

Domain Driven Design (DDD) by Eric Evans is the best way I know to consider the domain architecture. The concepts contained in DDD allow us to form consistent and understandable architectures that have more staying power than the implementation architecture. I have been disappointed that DDD is not more widely used to inform solution structures.

On Design

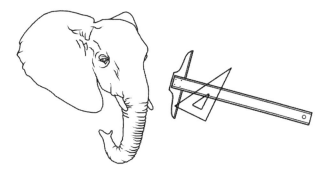

In the last chapter we talked about the importance of architecture, and the themes of domain architecture and implementation architecture. And I said then that in my mind, design is very close to architecture. To me, architecture is high-level design, the biggest design, how I think about the biggest pieces of a project. I know that is not a politically acceptable definition, but it is how I think about it.

Design is something that goes all the way down, from the architectural level to the smallest level of detail.

A system always has a design; you can't have something that isn't designed, because design is how a thing is put together, how we think about it. It consists of a series of decisions.

Design is always present in any system. How conscious and appropriate is that design? Now that is the real question!

Is your design something that is informing your activities? Is it informing the work you are doing? Or is the design something that's there to be worked around—are you trying to get around the design?

"We should do it this way, but it's not working very well so let's just do it this other way."

When you work around the design, rather than taking the time to revisit it, you lose some tremendous opportunities; tremendous opportunities for improvement, tremendous opportunities for making things better as things change, because if there is anything we know about the world, it is that things are going to change.

So how do you know if we have a good design? First of all, let's be practical: a good design is something that people recognize—it's like the old saw about the question, "What is art?" The classic answer to which is, "I don't know, but I know it when I see it." In the same way, people do recognize when a design is good.

But beyond than that simple, gut-level reaction, there are things you can look for: a good design is something that retains its shape, retains its character as things in the project change—and remember, things always change. In agile development, change comes more and more rapidly, and because change is more rapid, then design becomes more important—not less!

In that sense, design is something we think of as *so important* that we want to do it all the time. That is what refactoring is all about. Refactoring says: When the design is starting to get out of date, we will refactor the code to conform to a new design. And we want to do that why? Because design constrains how we think about things. It constrains how we look at the world. Improving design improves our thinking.

One of my tests for how a software team is doing is this: Can every person on the team talk about the design? Can they talk about how the system hangs together? If they cannot, they are probably in trouble and have a lot of learning to do.

I come from a background of modeling. We use modeling to talk about design, but modeling is just a different language to use to talk about design. I was on a team once where we built three-dimensional models of the design and had them hooked together with little strings, and we hung them in the middle of the team room, from the ceiling. So if we wanted to talk about the design, we could look up and see our visualization of the design, and point to things, and talk about them. In other projects I've been on, there have been parts of the design that lived on white boards that were always right there, visible to the whole team. So I could always tell if people were really using design as a tool, because they would go right up to the white board and talk about it and say, "See, its working here!" or "The design isn't working here. Why is that? Is it because we don't understand the problem, or does the design need to be improved? Or do we not understand the problem in terms of how we are thinking about solutions?"

This activity we call design is, I think, the primary activity of software development. The primary activity is not coding. We now know that coding on most projects comprises less than 10% of the work, and believe me, that figure has been going down throughout my career. Over the years I spend less and less and less time coding.

With the languages and tools we have available now, whole sets of problems go away because the languages embody a design, a way of thinking about how we do things. If you look at how languages these days do collections, for instance, you iterate all the collections and that's basically a method on collections. But we had to do all that by hand before and set up indices and iterate over them and increment the index and look for end conditions—and there were lots of bugs. Language designers now build these things into languages, so those kinds of bugs don't happen.

But that is not the main reason you want to use these tools. The main reason you want to use these evolved language tools is that you are upping the level of abstraction in your discourse. You are upping the level of thinking about problems. When you have collections of things, you are now free to think purely in terms of going over the collection of things and doing stuff to it.

A great deal of functional programming is all about how to do that in a way that is very, very fast and resilient to scaling. There are rules around that, and what are those rules? Those rules are really design patterns.

Patterns are standard approaches, standard designs that solve common problems—but they are designs. If you don't understand patterns at this level; then you are missing an opportunity to learn about higher level designs, higher level abstractions. If you do understand this, you can bring the conversations within the team and between the team and with people outside the team to a higher level of abstraction and get closer to solving the problem.

If you can't talk about the design of your system, then you've got some work to do, because if you can't talk about it, you can't be conscious about it. You can't really understand what's going on until you can talk about design as problem solving at a high level of abstraction, and not just talk about it in terms of the code.

To me that is one of the disadvantages I see now in the open source community—almost everything is talked about in terms of example code. Well, that tells you how a system works, but it is very, very difficult to convey the design of a system and to think about the system in a sophisticated way.

Spend more time with design, spend more time understanding the design you are working with, and learn to communicate at the design level, at the abstract level, with your fellow workers, and you'll write better software.

On Language

Language wars

Anyone who has been in the software business as long as I have has been through some pretty serious language wars. People get very passionate about computer languages: what they can do, what they can't do, and all that jazz. Why is that?

We have to invest a lot of time and energy to become good in a language, and we like to protect our investments. We have also had positive experiences that reinforce our love for, and comfort in, a language: we use languages to solve problems, and most of us have experienced a language feature making some problem that had seemed very difficult suddenly seem very easy. What's not to love about that? So we grow passionate....

I agree that it is important for people who write code to get good at some of the languages they use. I've been in the software business for over 50 years now, and for the first 35 of those I was actively programming. Interestingly enough, though, I only spent serious time in three languages: assembly language, Smalltalk and Java.

When I started out there weren't a lot of choices outside of assembly language and Fortran. As other languages started to come out I dabbled in lot of them: I did little PL/I, some JOVIAL, a little bit of C and C++, but very little because I never liked them. I found those languages cumbersome, and I didn't enjoy working with them… so I didn't.

Because I had my own consulting business, I discovered early on that I didn't necessarily need to be expert in the most popular languages—I just needed to be expert in a language that enough people wanted to use that I could land a consulting job! Sometimes it even helped to be the rare expert in a less popular language.

I specialized in Smalltalk development for a number of years, and people were always advising me, "You should do C++! There are ten times as many projects using C++ as there are projects using Smalltalk!"

To which I would say, "But there is only one of me, and I only need one or two customers at any given time."

For me, it was important to work in a language I understood and enjoyed. You have to look at yourself, figure out what you want to do and how you want to feel about it, and take action based on your findings.

Don't change languages the way you change your shirts

When a young developer says to me, "I know 25 languages!" I don't believe them, because if a person has taken the time to learn that many languages, then they certainly haven't taken the time to get to know any one of them well!

I am not a great believer in jumping from language to language to language. I think it is better practice to dive into one language and learn to be exceptionally good at it.

I read manuals for a lot of languages, and I would say that I am familiar with—that I am acquainted with—many languages. Lately I have been getting acquainted with Scala, because I think Scala is an interesting language. I have spent time in Ruby. I can say that I am familiar with these languages, but I certainly don't have enough facility with them to know their strengths and weaknesses in great detail. I think you should know that for the languages in which you specialize—I think you need to be expert in the languages you work in.

At the same time, I believe in pair programming, and you don't necessarily have to be an expert in a language to pair effectively with someone who is. You may not be able to write code fluently in it, but often times you can do enough to provide value, and if you can't, then chances are the project has even bigger problems— because if the language is driving everything, if all the decisions are based around the language, then you are not really looking at the underlying design problem anyway.

You should know the language you're working in well enough that the problem is not the language. You should know the language well enough that all you are concerned about is the problem the language can solve.

If you do know your language and you are working on a problem and language keeps getting in the way, then I would suggest you may not be working in the right language, and in today's world there are plenty of choices.

The Tower of Babel

Having so many choices can present both a problem and an opportunity; it's a problem because developers often don't really know any one language well enough, and it's an opportunity because you might just find exactly the right language to solve the problem.

I have learned enough about Lisp to know that some developers have done Lisp implementation on the server side and it has clearly out-performed a Java implementation of the same thing. Using a language like Scala to solve performance problems of a different kind can be a very useful thing to do as well—in fact it can run on top of Java and make it faster and easier to use in more environments. These are the kinds of solutions that having a basic familiarity with lots of languages enables—you know enough to think to use them, even if they are not your bread and butter.

Back to basics

There are a lot of languages out there you could learn, but have you learned the basic programming concepts?

If you don't know objects well, for example, I believe it will be impossible for you to build a maintainable system. Notice I said a maintainable system. Objects you can test allow you to build systems which are maintainable. By maintainable I mean that I, as the maintainer, can walk into code that you have written, figure out what's wrong, fix it, test it, and know that it will work.

Now, that is theoretically possible in any language, but I believe objects give you a way to encapsulate your thinking and actually achieve this in practice.

Similarly, have you learned functional programming? Do you know what functions are and how to use them?

One of the things I didn't realize in 1983, when I was learning Smalltalk, was that functional programming concepts were built in, so we just didn't talk about them. We used them, but it was just part of what we did—sometimes I wonder about how dense I can be!

I didn't enjoy working in Java anywhere near as much as I enjoyed Smalltalk, but it took me a long time to realize that this was because Java didn't support functional programming in any way that made sense to me. I knew this at a gut level, but it wasn't until much later that I could articulate it.

So you need to learn a language and get good at it, but then you should also come to understand the way it works. Figure out how it does stuff. Teach some classes in it if you can—that is the best way to explore the space of understanding a language.

And remember, you don't need to keep up with the Joneses of the world; languages last for a long time in our business, so you don't need to be worry about keeping abreast of the latest language fad. That's not what we need in programming; we need depth of experience and depth of knowledge. Depth will make you more money in the long run, give you more satisfaction, and make you a better developer.

Easy come, easy go

If you look at the people who signed the Agile Manifesto, you'll find that a majority of them were involved in a programming language called Smalltalk. Around two thirds of the founders of the agile movement were actively using Smalltalk as a tool at the time. This is significant because at that point of time, the market for Smalltalk development was a tiny percentage of the market for development in other languages like C++.

So what is that about? Is it happenstance? Just dumb luck? I don't think so.

I was one of those people involved in agile projects in 1987, and we had Smalltalk projects in development that were successfully delivering full tested functionality every six weeks. The first Scrum project was Smalltalk based. So, what was it about Smalltalk that made it so compelling, and is there something to be learned from that?

Smalltalk was a language that made it very easy to build what we now call domain specific language. Today people do this all the time in languages like Ruby and Scala, but at the time it was a new concept, and Smalltalk made it very easy to do. That became a way to talk about solving problems, and since we now had a way to talk about problem solving, we talked about it a lot more!

I still believe good object oriented development looks a lot like what we used to do in Smalltalk, and I am actually disappointed in some of the code I see these days, in how little flavor is actually in the code.

Back then, those of us in the Smalltalk community would go onto the Usenet mailing lists and talk in terms of solving problems, and we'd look at the C++ mailing lists and joke about how those "C++ people" were always talking about "pointers" and "memory references," what would the compiler do here, and which database to use, and so on, while we "Smalltalk people" were always talking about the problem. We were trying to get to a point where once you implemented a solution, anyone could just read the code and understand exactly what it did. That was something else unique about Smalltalk at the time—it was eminently readable. Some of that was the syntax, which was absurdly simple—I could teach someone the syntax of Smalltalk in 20 minutes. For example, Smalltalk doesn't just have a list of parameters. Instead, you intersperse the parameters with the name and the method.

So instead of saying:

make rectangle (width, height)

you would say:

make a rectangle of (width: 50px) and (height: 50px)

When you read this kind of code, the code is telling you exactly what is going on—this was remarkable, especially when you remember that Smalltalk is now 35 years old. Even today, in most modern languages, when you read a method it's next to impossible to figure out what the parameters mean and what the method is doing unless you actually go look at the declaration of the method. But I don't care about definitions and declarations. It's the use of it that I want to be able to read when I am trying to understand what is going on in the code!

In Smalltalk it was very easy to write what we call intention-revealing method names. And because we did that, and because there was a lot of top down development in Smalltalk because of the way it worked, it was so easy to write stuff down that the system was always telling you what needed to be done next. So the system literally kept the low-level, detail backlog for you, all the little things that needed to be done.

It didn't do this by keeping a list of things to do. Instead what happened was that you would run the system, and the system would stop and say, "You need to fix this now." So you would fix the something and then tell the system to go on running. Development and test were an integrated whole.

Now, we eventually discovered that this wasn't quite enough, that we also needed to make sure we didn't break anything from the past. So we would have to write some additional tests. But even the test writing had that same flavor to it: You wrote the test, the test would access code that wasn't written yet, so you would write the test and the code would break and it would stop right there and say, "What do you want me to do?" Then you would say "Do this!" and then tell the system to run.

So Smalltalk created an environment and a way of working that made it incredibly easy to find things. Any time there was any token, a method name, a variable name, whatever it was—and there were only three kinds of syntactic elements in Smalltalk, so it was simple—all you would have to do is mark that and say, "Explain this." And the system would tell you everything it knew: where it was used, where it was defined, how it was defined. It was wonderful to use in that regard. You always knew what to do next.

This was a problem for my wife. Since everything in Smalltalk would only take 10 or 15 minutes to do, things that were really small and bite-sized, and since so you always had these little things to do, I kept saying, "Oh, just five more minutes, dear!" And then one thing would lead to another until suddenly I'd look up and find that I'd been at it for hours and hours, much to her annoyance. So Smalltalk could be hard on a spouse!

I have idealized Smalltalk here, and certainly there were things that weren't quite right, and things that it didn't do well, of course. But in terms of development, and solving problems, and really getting at the essence of a problem and modeling it and having it execute so that you really knew what was true and what was possible, I have never seen anything that compares to Smalltalk. Ruby is as close to a similar language as I have seen, but I found myself not so happy with Ruby because it gives me a lot of choices but not enough guidance.

It all comes back again to just this: I really want to solve problems. I am less concerned about the computer. I want tools to help me solve the problem that's in front of me, and not to have to worry about things like what kind of database to use.

Why do good technologies sometimes fail?

That's an interesting question. Smalltalk was a radical shift, for two reasons: first, it was object oriented, which no one knew anything about back then, and second, the syntax wasn't just C. To me that was a lot of its power, but it freaked people out. There was lot of resistance to it, and C had a much larger market share so people wanted to just go to C++, because it was a smaller move, and to their minds a much easier move. And early Smalltalk systems weren't as performant. It turned out you really needed 32 bit machines and this was when those were first starting to come into play. The other event that affected the adoption of Smalltalk was that Java came out, and Java had a lot of industry support and good marketing. There is an interesting bit of mythology, and I am not sure if it's true, that Microsoft actually looked at Smalltalk and were very close to making a decision to use Smalltalk, but they decided not to. And that is how the world goes: If someone like Bill Gates had decided to put Smalltalk in place, who knows what would have happened?

To me it's not so much about the rightness of the technology. There is a lot of serendipity involved.

Pair Programming

My first experience was with pair programming, like many people's, was not so good. The learning curve for pair programming is steep, and a lot of people decide after too-brief exposure that it's not for them, and this is unfortunate. So even though I didn't have a great experience my first time pairing, I kept trying, and it has kept getting better. Now it is how I prefer to work.

What is the point of pairing? Do we do it because we are going to write code faster? Well, there is a little bit of that. In her book, *Pair Programming Illuminated*, Laurie Williams cites data that indicates pairs produce about 15% more code than two individual contributors working separately.

But the objective is not solely to write more code; the objective is to write better code. When pairing is successful, you find yourself writing better code because someone is helping you. You help each other. You elevate the level of shared knoweldge.

I like to set up pairing so that one person is always in charge. If you're doing agile development and using a task board, then one person goes up to the task board, pulls a task, holds up the card and says, "I'd like to pair with someone on this task. Who wants to pair with me?"

The person who starts the pairing session in this way is the one who is in charge, the owner of the task. They usually start being the one typing. The other person is the note taker.

One of the questions that comes up often is, how long should two people pair together? The answers to that question can be extreme: Some people answer that a pair should team up for an entire sprint, while others think they should pair for an hour then switch partners. The right question is, where's the sweet spot for you? For your team? Is there one?

I have tried many permutations of pairing, and find that if you switch pairs about every five hours, that is where the knowledge gains level out. That is the sweet spot. So switching off pairs every half-day seems to be about right.

One way I've seen this work well is for the person who plucked the task from the board and became its owner would stay with the task, and the other developer would switch halfway through the day.

If the task lasted longer than a day and it was time to switch a second time, then the original owner might switch out as well. Sometimes we had hard tasks that might take three or four days to do—which is a very large task indeed, and not advised—and over that length of time a number of people might cycle through working on the task as part of a pair. When we worked this way, we ensured there was always continuity by having one person from the previous pairing remaining on the task.

Those are the logistics of pairing, but people often ask me, what are the actual mechanics of pairing? How does it really work?

Well, I like to think of it using a race car analogy: one person should always be the navigator and the other person should be the driver. The navigator is the one taking notes, keeping track of details and making sure the pair doesn't forget anything. The driver is the one doing the typing, the one working on the machine.

There have been times when I've had two people working on a machine at the same time. I've even had some experience running a mouse while someone else ran the keyboard, and that was kind of interesting, because a few times it actually worked very well! In general it doesn't, but we did try it just to see what it was like—just for fun. You never know until you try!

The navigator keeps an eye on what's going on, and their main job is to observe and be a sounding board for what the driver is doing. If the navigator doesn't understand what's going on, they need to pipe up and say, "What are you doing? Why are you doing that?" Then the driver, the person who's actually doing the coding, needs to explain their actions right then. It isn't sufficient for them just to say, "Well, let me work for two hours and then I'll show you what I did." That's not pair programming! When you're engaged in pair programming, there should be constant interaction.

The navigator also does things like writing notes about what the pair is doing and why, including documenting tests. In good pairing situations, those notes are kept right there in the code, because the navigator gets the keyboard too—the pair does switch off who is inputting. Having the navigator's notes close at hand helps give the next person to pair on the task some guidance about what's happening and what still needs to happen.

You drive for a while, and then you navigate. Then you switch again. But how often should that switching back and forth within the pair happen?

If you are doing test-driven development—which of course I recommend that you do—then writing a test and writing the code for that test typically takes less than half an hour. I've seen it take as little as 10 minutes. So you might switch the navigator and the driver between testing and coding. Personally I've gotten to the point now where I don't type very well, and so I navigate much more than I type, and that works out pretty well. You've got to look at the circumstances to see what works. Try things out.

One thing that never works is when one person types most of the time because they've got a big "thing" they want to do, and they want to get it done without the back and forth. That's not true pairing, because if you don't have that recurring interchange, that back-and-forth. You will not be getting the true benefit and power of pair programming.

And what is that power? That power is doing things better while writing less code. Sometimes you start writing, and your pair partner says, "Why are you doing that?" and you say, "Well, I'm doing it because I needed xyz." And your partner says, "Hey, there is already a method that does that." Or the answer might be, "I'm doing this because I've gotten lost." Or the answer might be a quick little sketch of a sequence diagram you draw up to explain what's going on. That kind of in-the-moment communication before you actually write the code is very important to writing better, more conscious code.

Another thing that happens in coding is that you can get lost. One of you has an idea and starts coding, exploring that idea. But if, as so often happens, the idea starts to go away, or you get lost, if you're by yourself it it very easy to spend a lot of time getting lost and going into the ditch. In a pair, the navigator's job is to notice that kind of thing, and to question how you got into the ditch? Questioning not in an accusatory way, but an interested way. "Why are you doing that? Explain it to me so I can learn." Maybe you are both confused and decide you need to explore.

We all have had the experience of trying to explain something we think is a great idea, and in that process discovering that it doesn't work at all. Has that happened to you, or is it just me?

That's the kind of thing we are looking for in pairing. We are looking for dynamic, real-time code review. In a pair, you are looking at the code as it's being written, you are talking about it, you are clarifying, you are coming up with a better name for a method or a variable because it more closely captures what you need. Maybe there is little refactoring going on—refactoring is an interesting time for creativity, and two people can definitely help each other with that.

All those things happen during a pairing session, so even though the quantity of code written per hour is not much greater—or is even the same—the actual quality and suitability of that code is typically much, much higher.

Learning in pairs: Why two heads are six times better than one

Your own learning curve is something I consider very personal: how you think, how I think, those are different. But when it comes down to the code level, when it comes down to how we learn from and learn within our implementations, then it's very useful to have other people involved. At that level, pair programming is a practice I consider to be a learning tool.

Yes, the practice of pair programming will help us produce code with fewer errors, but why is that? It is because we help each other catch things, we learn from each other constantly, and the code learns with us.

When I consult on a software project, I'll ask to pair with individuals just to learn more about what they are doing and how they are doing it. It's a great way for me to learn about the team and its issues, and a way for the team to learn, and we help each other by each bringing in ideas coming from outside the pair as well. We have a rich interaction, and the code of course gets better. It gets better as a result of us looking at things from these different points of view and bringing the synergy of human interaction into play.

No More Bugs

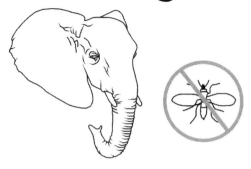

People in the software industry are always talking about bugs. We have bug tracking systems, we have bug triage, we have all these things around bugs—but do we ever really think about what bugs are? How they got there? How we can avoid ending up with more of them?

It is my belief that we as an industry have been so complacent about bugs that we believe all software has to be full of them. The mythology of computer software holds that all software systems have to have their bugs. I don't think that is true.

Imagine a world without bugs. Or at least imagine a world with an order of magnitude fewer bugs. I would suggest this goal isn't really difficult to attain.

So how do we go about it?

First, we want to be conscious about bugs, to really think about them: What are they there for? What do we mean when we say there is a bug?

There are three kinds of bugs:

The first kind of bug is an *error*. There is something wrong within the software system, such that it is not doing what we wanted it to do. That is a bug.

The second kind of bug is what we call an *enhancement*. The system isn't broken, but it doesn't do quite what we wanted it to do—not exactly, not yet. That is an enhancement bug.

The third type of bug is a *feature* bug—it's not something broken, but something the system should do but that it doesn't do. Often as new features are introduced, we find our system doesn't do things that need doing to support these new features. This kind of feature bug is something that you really do want to have as a feature of the system you're building, but as of now it isn't there yet. As is said: "That's not a bug it's an undocumented feature!"

It is true that on some level no system is ever complete, and so in that sense bugs, or at least feature bugs, will always be a part of any system.

But let's set aside feature bugs for now and focus on the kinds of bugs that throw us errors, bugs that are causing your software to misbehave.

In my experience, it is entirely possible to build systems that exhibit very little "buggy" behavior. How do we do that? If we adopt a lean way of thinking, we think about reducing the feedback time in our system. In this light, we view a bug as some behavior of the system that has escaped past when it was put into the system. What we want to do is reduce the time from when we learn this has happened to when the bug gets fixed.

The teams that decide fixing bugs is of the utmost importance get to where they want to be by reducing the cycle time, reducing the feedback time from when a bug is introduced to when it is fixed. Not the time from when the bug is found in the system, but when it was introduced—there's a big difference.

When you find a bug, you should use your source control system to go back and find the point in time when the bug was introduced. Now, you may ask: Why go to all that trouble, as opposed to just fixing it when and where you find it and moving on?

Because by looking at exactly when and where the bug occurred, you learn something about why it occurred, and this is how you learn how to write fewer bugs.

That's the real goal: to write fewer bugs.

What do most development teams do with bugs? A customer finds a bug in our system, reports it, and what do we do? We do bug triage. Is it an "important" bug? What makes a bug important? Typically, a bug that causes our customer to lose data would be considered important. We would fix that bug right away. Or is it a bug that our favorite customer is complaining about? We fix that bug because of a characteristic of the environment.

But if we're really trying to learn how to write fewer bugs, we shouldn't care about the bug's relative importance. In that sense, there is no difference between the high priority bug and low priority bug—they are both things that didn't behave the way we thought they should have behaved.

Doing bug triage in just a colossal waste of time in terms of learning how to write fewer bugs.

How can this be so? The best projects I've worked on, we didn't do bug triage at all. On one agile project, a team of 12 people worked for 18 months to deliver a product, and six months after the customer took delivery, exactly one bug had been reported.

We did it by making fixing bugs our highest priority. Whenever a bug showed up, the next person who was free (meaning they had finished their current task) would take on the bug. The bug's priority was naturally higher than other work on the task board at the time. It wasn't higher than the current task—whatever you were currently working on, you would not be interrupted by the bug—but since tasks typically took a day at most, someone on the team would get to the bug very quickly.

You would fix the bug and write new tests, yes, but the most important part of fixing a bug was that you would talk about how the bug got there. Having a lot of unit tests helps a lot, but really it's that questioning attitude, this belief that fixing bugs is the highest priority work.

When we don't fix bugs until six months after we write them, then the learning opportunity is lost. We learn from our mistakes by reducing the length of the feedback loop from when the code is checked in, to when the bug is exposed, and if we can get that cycle length down with unit testing, then we can learn about how not to write bugs, and again, that is the real goal: to write software without bugs.

There are companies in Japan that have also reported that kind of performance. And we think about that kind of performance in space shuttle software. So it is possible!

Now, when we have systems and environments that work like that, how does that change the work? How does that change what we think about? How does that charge what we do?

The defining characteristic is that the team spends its time looking forward, they are not looking back. If you have ever driven a car, you know that facing forward works lot better than looking over your shoulder all the time.

The same applies in software development: if you are looking six months back, looking at things you wrong a year ago, digging into code you haven't looked at in a long, long time, then you are living in the past. You want to be moving forward all the time, having that attitude that says, "Bugs? We don't need no stinkin' bugs!"

You need to have the attitude that a bug is something you squash immediately. You don't prioritize it, you don't put it in a backlog, you just squash it. This way you don't even have to worry about bugs, and all of that neck-straining, backward-facing work completely goes away.

This makes you more agile in terms of what you an building, which means the team can be more focused on the work, and that work will be much happier for everyone.

Cost of fixing bugs

Some folks will counter this attitude about bugs by saying that all this testing, all this bug fixing, will cost too much. It does not appear to be so. I see places with whole teams doing nothing but bug fixing—big bug backlogs that require time and money to keep up, prioritization, verification, triage, purging, communication to customers, reduced feature development time.

I would love to see more companies keep good track and actually know how much bugs cost them and, in particular, accounting for the cost of the bugs against the team that wrote them. This would be a major change in measuring productivity of teams!

Debugging

When you've got bugs, how do you find them?

The tools and technology available for debugging have grown considerably better over the years, but it's not clear to me that the actual art and practice of debugging has gotten any better.

Many years ago when I started out in software, compilations would take about 24 hours, and so debugging was a very different kind of operation. You did a lot of desk checking, and you learned how to put a lot of indicators into your code so you could see what was going on. This way, when things went wrong you could look at the indicators and know where you were.

It all came to a culmination for me when I was working with microprocessors. At that point in time there were no development systems for microprocessors, so there was no way to single-step these things. You had to do all of your debugging based on evidence—side effects that the processors left lying around. It was difficult.

I was working at a small company at the time, where there were only two of us doing most of the software development. My colleague was an excellent developer, but he wrote very convoluted code.

Some time after he had been moved out to a separate project, I was charged with fixing a particular area, because we didn't have enough performance on this one bit of code he had written.

I spent a fair bit of time debugging and trying to find out what was going on. Finally, I gave up. I went to my bosses and said, "Look I can't do this, I need to take another approach."

To solve the problem, I ended up re-implementing the code. This time around, I built a little monitoring system and suddenly everything started working.

So sometimes debugging is really a matter of saying "Look, this code is not understandable the way it is, and we need to understand it better before we can debug it." Sometimes that means rewriting, which can be dangerous unless you have written tests. That's what re-factoring is about: not necessary changing the design, but changing the implementation to better understand the design.

I began to notice something, after this incident: the better the software developer, the more they re-wrote their code, and the clearer they were about what it was doing.

I recognized this recurring phenomenon of code; it didn't work right, then we re-wrote it and it did. In many cases, we accomplished this without really quite understanding what we had done differently the second time around—it just worked. Often it wasn't worth the time and effort to go in and try to understand why. Interesting, yes?

Debugging should really be an opportunity to understand your code better. With the growth of testing as a way of doing development, debugging becomes much less of a time sink. This is a good thing, because debugging isn't really a very efficient use of our time. We'd like to spend it on the really hairy problems, and not on the simpler problems that unit testing can solve for us.

It all circles back to good design, and using all the tricks we know to help us write better software.

The other side of it is that many, many bugs show up as a result of an early conception of an object that had some responsibilities, and those responsibilities grew too much. Now this is an old argument, about encapsulation, but for me it remains a very real argument because it has come out of my experience.

I noticed that when I had a complicated class that did a bunch of things, if I separated this complex class out into three or four classes, with each class doing fewer things, that the code became more reliable. It just worked better.

One can even argue that the real value of object oriented programming lies in its ease of maintenance. When debugging is easier, you constrain your fixes; you know you're not going to need to go outside of your boundaries. And with the addition of good coverage in unit testing, this makes for systems that are very, very robust.

Now, this does not solve problems having to do with the higher level design being inadequate, or the architecture that you picked being not quite up to the challenge. You may still have those issues, but notice how we've raised the complexity level quite a lot. The abstraction level is considerably higher, and so the tools we need to use to solve these higher order problems are a little different.

Where we have complex systems and emergent behavior, testing and experimentation is the only way to debug. We have to try things and see what they do—try this, try that. We try different paths through the code, then looked at the log files to see all the evidence that was laid bare around that path.

You need to make sure you are using the right tools at the right level; if you are debugging way down in the code, you shouldn't be having to create lots of log files laying it all out—I watch people put a lot of code like that into their systems, then turn around and wonder why the system is so slow!

If you're spending all your time writing out log files, then even if you have a good mechanism for turning the logging on and off, you can still add a lot of overhead. What happens then is that you have less system performance for very little gain—you are spending a lot of CPU cycles gathering information that is rarely relevant.

Now people argue that when this information is relevant that then you really need it. I would say yes, but look at the data. Isn't it easier, when a problem comes up, to put some stuff in then and there, to help you figure out what is going on? Usually developers have some idea what the issue is.

Or is it better in the long run to have some high level stuff with not much overheard that gives you enough context that now when a bug does show up you can reconstruct it? Figuring out how to do that is an art.

What we want to do is reduce the time we spend single-stepping the code and looking at it on that level, because it's such an incredibly bad use of both people time and computer time. So think about your level of abstraction when you're debugging, and what low-level testing you can implement to make those kind of bugs less likely.

Then you can think about the system: What's your architecture? Where and how are things hanging together? Because when you get there, reading and understanding the code itself will help you find those high level bugs more than any other technique.

The Zen of Automated Testing

My first job in software was as a tester, over 50 years ago, and that is something I still pride myself on. I can walk up to nearly any system and break it. For some reason, I think about the code differently than a lot of people do.

So let's think differently about this: How do we design a test strategy for our products in which the people spend their time doing the stuff people do best, letting the computers do what computers do best?

When I visit companies as a consultant I see some automated testing, but it's usually all at the GUI level. They use some sort of tool that captures the GUI, and write tests to test the entire system.

The problem with that approach is that it is inefficient: If you look at the utilization of the CPU, where is the CPU spending it's time for that kind of testing? For most modern applications, you will find that the CPU is spending most of its time in the database, or maybe in the operating system, or waiting on the network. This means that we are not actually using the computer to test our code—we are testing the database, over and over and over again.

Now, we do need that kind of testing, because we need to see the entire system, but it is actually a very inefficient way to test all of our code—and we really would like to test all of our code.

In their book *Agile Testing*, authors Janet Gregory and Lisa Crispin talk about testing in four quadrants. They talk about unit testing, what they call quadrant one, which for me means the testing the developers do on their own code. "Is the code doing what we think it should do?"

An interesting thing about automated testing is that it is not really about today's code. I don't know any developer who thinks that they are going to write bad code. Of course not! They are going to write good code! But it's the code you write today that breaks the code you wrote yesterday. Catching that breakage, that is the real purpose of automated testing.

The kind of automated testing that catches breakage is regression testing, and it is something you should do every day. The idea is to reduce the time from when a bug is introduced into the system until we fix it. This time can be reduced significantly by having that kind of testing going on all the time.

Quadrant two testing, in Crispin & Gregory terminology, is acceptance testing, story testing—you are testing behavior.

Acceptance testing asks: Is the code exhibiting the behavior we intend it to? You still want to automate acceptance testing, because you want to know when and if functionality gets broken—and sometimes it isn't due to the code that we wrote; it can occur just because a new library has been brought in, for example, or we have a new version of the database, and now something is broken. In that case all of our unit tests, all those developer-written unit tests which test the code we wrote, would still pass, but our acceptance tests might fail.

The third quadrant is exploratory testing, and that's the testing we would really like the QA people to be spending most of their time doing. This is an area in which automation doesn't really add a lot, except during set-up and tear-down. Automation can be very useful to get things going, to set up an environment, to get to a known state, but exploratory testing is going to use the power of the human being, human eyes looking at the problem from one angle and then another, trying to see it in as many ways as possible.

The last area, quadrant four, is a very specialized area. This has to do with scalability, security, all those "-ilities" that lie outside the system. Testing those requires specialized resources and often specialized knowledge.

So those are the four quadrants:

> *unit testing*
>
> *acceptance testing*
>
> *exploratory testing*
>
> *"-ility" testing*

Of the four quadrants, all but exploratory testing are best served with automation. Why have humans do the things that computers can do so much better? Let the humans focus their efforts where they really can add value.

White box, black box

Testing folks sometime talk about "white box" vs. "black box" testing. Let's consider this:

Yes, we want to look at the entire system and think about it as a black box. We can do black box testing, but what we really want to do is be efficient in all of our testing to make sure that for every line of code, for every conditional statement that we write, for every exception that could be thrown—that yes, we have a test for that. That kind of testing cannot be done in a black box, even theoretically. You have to do white box testing, which is what unit testing is really all about. I would argue that doing that kind of testing is very, very important to a successful software project.

Most people think of black box testing as "what we want to do here!" After all, it is what the customer sees. But consider an automobile. Can the lab-coated technician with his clipboard at the end of the production line actually find many of the potential bugs? Say a missing bolt holding the engine on the frame. Or would that bug only by found by the customer when they drive over a big pothole and the engine falls out? These kinds of bugs are only found on the production line as the car is assembled.

Unit Testing

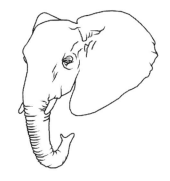

I get a big smile when I think about unit testing. Why? Because it's so much fun!

By unit testing, I mean the kind of testing developers do to make sure the code is doing what they think it should do. Unit testing is one of those things I really enjoy doing as developer, and it has proven itself to be incredibly useful over the years on all kinds of projects, big and small.

I started coding a long, long time ago, long before unit testing was even feasible, and since I learned to code without it, it is still hard for me sometimes, as much as I enjoy it—I want to dive right into the code!

But if you can teach yourself to do unit testing, what you will find is that you write less code, and you write better code.

Why is that?

Well, on one level, it's quite simple: You can't test bad code. Good code, code which is designed well, actually makes testing easier. So if your unit testing is proving difficult, then you probably have a design problem in your code.

This is an interesting point, because a lot of people will say, "Well, testing is about finding bugs," or "Testing is about regression."

And that is indeed one side of unit testing—making sure that the code you worked on today didn't break the code you or someone else wrote yesterday, or last week, or last year.

But the other side of unit testing is about actually improving the design and making the code better, because if you can't test your code, then you have a design problem, not a testing problem.

To be a conscious unit tester, you have to continually ask yourself questions like:

Where is the CPU spending its time?

Is the CPU spending its time actually running your code?

Or is the CPU just spending its time doing something else, like running a database?

The best project I ever worked on was one for which we engaged in massive unit testing. We wrote tests for every line of code we wrote. So for every 100 lines of Java code we wrote, we have about 230 lines of test code. A lot of people who saw us doing this would throw up their hands and exclaim over how much productivity we were losing by writing this many tests. But we weren't losing any productivity at all—quite the opposite.

Why? Because we were quickly finding all of the bugs, all of those things that you would otherwise spend hours finding down the road, or trying to find, if you were lucky.

The beauty of unit testing is that when an error gets injected into the system, you discover it right away, and you discover it automatically, before something breaks and sends you on a hunting mission.

Pair programming is a great way to help one another learn about unit testing. So many unit tests have been developed during pair programming that I've come to believe that it's hands-down the best way to do unit testing.

You may not be able to do unit testing that way if you're working in a legacy code base, but if you are just coding up a little piece of something that's brand new, even if it's inside of a legacy system, you can do your own unit testing.

I will even go so far as to suggest that you may find that this practice changes how you code and how you think about code. What you will be doing is asking yourself, "What should this code do?" before you write the code, and when you start with that salient question, one of the things we all experience who have done this, is that you will find you actually write less code to solve the problem.

And we want to write less code! Less code is a good thing! It's less code to maintain, less code to have bugs—there are all these benefits to writing less code.

So use unit testing not just to write fewer bugs, but to help you write less code, and to solve design problems.

Refactoring

Our conceptualization of any design problem changes over time. It changes even as we solve the problem, and we don't always acknowledge that in our processes.

We think that solving a problem means that we have understood it. Not really; solving a problem once only means is that we understood it just enough to solve it that one way.

We don't make the most of what we have learned during that first pass at a solution unless we look at it again. See, by solving the problem the first time, we have changed our understanding of how that problem could be solved. We have arrived at a deeper understanding of the problem, one based on experience. So ask yourself: now what would happen if we went back to the same problem and looked at it with fresh eyes? Would we come up with an even better, cleaner, stronger, more scalable, less breakable solution? What do you think?

I've mentioned elsewhere that being fully conscious involves oscillating frequently between the detail-level and the big picture. Refactoring is a discipline that creates particularly harmonious oscillation patterns between the code and the team of people building it. Refactoring is all about making your code and your team more conscious.

Often times when you are first getting your code to work, that is all you focus on: getting it to work. At that stage of the game, getting it to work can be enough of a problem. You might have written some tests to help you get it to work, and that is very useful because those tests give you a record of how you decided it would work, what it means for the code to work, and that is very useful for the next step, which is to refactor—to go back and clean up your code.

I've heard plenty of developers express the view that cleaning up the code is useless. "The code works, so why clean it up? It's wasted effort. If it breaks, we'll fix it."

There are two reasons to refactor: One is that as the code changes, as it evolves, it will become harder and harder to clean up down the line. The earlier you clean up your work, the better. But the second and I think more compelling argument in favor of refactoring early and often is that you want to take advantage of the learning opportunity provided by the coding work you just performed.

Refactoring is about much more than clean-up. To me refactoring is the time to sit back and contemplate, to stroke the beard—if you don't have a beard you can stroke your bare chin. You might pretend you have a beard, just to see what it feels like to be old and wise <grin>.

I think all refactoring should be done in pairs. Refactoring by oneself is useful, but nowhere near as much learning occurs as when you pair up. Try asking yourselves some questions:

How did we do?

What are we really trying to do?

What are the patterns that are showing up here?

I find it very difficult to think about those broader themes and motifs when I'm deep in the middle of solving the problem itself. When I'm up to my elbows in code, solving an immediate problem, well, I may want to just hack on in there—hacking is very useful in terms of getting an immediate problem solved.

But hacking is much more powerful if you get in the habit of afterward sitting back and taking what you've built and looking at it again. Now that we know what we know and have solved the problem one way, how do we make the solution move closer to what the real problem is—now that we fully we understand it?

Now, at the lowest level the refactoring is quite simple. You comb through your code and look for patterns and inconsistencies: Are we using the same method in two places for two different things when really it's one thing? Much of refactoring involves the examination of these low-level design practices. That's the lowest level of refactoring.

Then there are the higher levels. Wiki creator Ward Cunningham keeps a thesaurus at hand. While looking at the name of a method or the name of an object or variable he likes to look it up and ask, "What is this thing really? Could we give it a better name, a name which describes it even more accurately?" Right now you know exactly what the name means, because you just wrote the code. It's fresh in your mind. But when you look at the code a year or two later, will the name you gave that object or method or variable still resonate? Will it make sense? And when someone new to the team looks at the code you wrote, will the name make your code self-explanatory, or at least easy to understand?

That learning that happened as we solved the problem, that is what gives us enough information to name it more concisely. And that is why there are levels of improvement that can only be achieved through refactoring.

It is an interesting dynamic, this flow of information between the system and the team building the system. The system is learning more about what we are doing and that is embodied in the code. At the same time, the team is learning more about what's going on at individual level, at the team level, at the code level, and at the process level.

As team members and pairs you are helping each other learn new ways to do things, and as your team starts to share more learning, as the information about how to solve a problem is more widely distributed, your team grows more dynamic, less constrained by knowledge that resides with just one person.

All of those things are happening at once, and if we don't take the time for refactoring, to embody that learning in ourselves and embody it in the team, then we are missing a golden opportunity.

Let's be very clear about this: data that researchers have collected indicate that the highest-performing agile teams are the ones that are better at learning. I've seen very good teams that knew how to learn together and how the code learns and how they learn as individuals and how they learn as a team—I've seen teams like these take on problems that they didn't know anything about, take them on just because they are interested in learning. And of course if you are interested in learning about something, it's a lot easier to learn about it isn't it? And so those teams would bid for the work just for the chance to learn from it.

The team that says, "We don't know anything about Scala, therefore we want to take on a Scala project." That's the team that is fully conscious, the team that learns well together, the team that enjoys and seeks out opportunities to learn. And if you're on that team, you become more valuable. You become more valuable as an individual to your team, and you become more valuable as an individual in your profession. And your life becomes a lot more interesting and a lot more fun.

On Being
Quiet

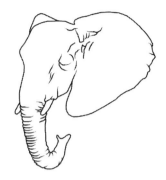

The industry we are in is always pushing us to do more, always wanting to us to be active, to over-commit. We are given "stretch goals" to keep us moving, doing and acting. But that leaves us feeling behind, and that continuous state of feeling behind does not really work very well for us in the long run.

If the feeling of being behind is something going on inside of me, inside my consciousness, then it's going to spill out and it's going to affect what's going on in the work, in the software. When I'm in a rush I'm not going to take quite as much time as I should to look at something, I'm not going to reflect on what I'm doing, and I'm not going to have a very introspective view on my own process for doing it.

We need the outward view, but we also need the look inside—both the breathing out and the breathing in. We require both of those modalities to be active to get the work done.

What can we do about it?

How do we do both in a world that's driving us all the time to hurry up and reach for more? We do it by slowing down. The paradox of course is that it seems like we'll do less when we slow down, but in fact we get more done. We don't get more done in the sense of churning out more lines of code, but we get more done in terms of number of lines of codes we keep. This is because things you write in a hurry are the things you will later find are broken.

In this sense, productivity is really all about doing less, and how we can learn to do less and accomplish more. If you don't reflect, if you don't have enough time to look at what's going on around and inside of you, to see what is happening, then you actually never learn how to get better at writing code—you might get faster, but you'll never get better. When you slow down you do write less code, but since you also write fewer bugs, the sum total of your effective output over time will be greater.

So how do we do that? One of my favorite personal methods is very simple. I'll go to meetings a little bit early, just to give myself enough time to breathe and think. I believe we should run our meetings more like we did when we were in grade school. At my grade school, the bell would ring at five to the hour, and then we would take another five minutes to move between classrooms. But out here in the world, the meeting goes from 9 to 10, and it lasts until 10 or even after, and the next meeting starts at 10 on another floor of the building. So there is no time—there is actually negative time. You need more time just to get from here to there, let alone taking a moment to think about things like, "What does the information I just absorbed mean for myself? For my project?" So give yourself a little more time if you can. If you need to, pipe up and request that meetings be scheduled with some gap time, for the benefit of those who must move between them. You can take some time at the beginning or the end of a meeting, or even in the middle of one. I've been known to stop meetings and say to everybody: "Just breathe, three times. In. Out. In. Out. In. Out." Three deep breaths can do amazing things.

There are other ways to slow down, some of which are entirely up to you. Do you think you are being productive just because you are checking email every five minutes? Try checking it every hour. Find a way to regulate that kind of behavior. When you go have a cup of coffee, go have a cup of coffee! Don't rush, gulping the cup of coffee in the middle of going from here to there— have a cup of coffee and take all the time you need to drink it.

How do you slow down enough? How do you get quiet? For me personally, it took many years to get into the habit of regular meditation practice, but daily meditation has had the largest impact of anything on my ability to be fully present, to be wherever I am. To be in the middle of doing something, and be fully conscious of what I'm doing. Even if you don't meditate, the brief moments you can take at the beginning of a meeting, or when you come in to work in the morning , where you sit down and say, "Okay what am I going to do today?" Maybe you don't have anything important on your plate to do that day, but you can still show up. Bringing even that level of consciousness and intention to bear can elevate your work habits.

To me a great deal of being conscious is taking care to simply show up. The great deal of how we are is as a result of our past history and what happened to us, how we think about things, and most of us have been on automatic pilot so long because we have gone on rushing until our bodies literary have trouble knowing how to slow down. The consequence is that we miss what is really going on.

This stuff isn't easy. To me, this is the practice of a lifetime.

Personality Types

How do we know how we operate? The essence of consciousness is about that—what do we know about ourselves?

There's a tool that I've used to help me make some amazing discoveries about myself. Some of you, many of you probably, have heard of something called Myers-Briggs personality classification system. We find that a lot of places primarily use it to help people learn that not everyone operates the same way. An example of one of the dimensions of Myers-Briggs is whether you tend to make decisions out of your thinking body—you think about things to make decisions—or you make decisions more out of your feeling self, your emotional body.

And different people have different sorts of degrees of that, which is particularly interesting to me. When I originally did Myers-Briggs testing I would always test out as what's called a "T" or "thinking" person. I finally got together years later with some experts in the field and while we were talking about this aspect I said, "Oh, yeah, I'm a 'T'" and they just laughed. It was so obvious to them I was not a "T". And I now know that I'm more an "F"—that I'm on the "feeling" side of that dimension, and it's how I make decisions.

It was interesting learning this about myself, and to learn that other people don't do things the same way that I do. Some people are introverts, some people are extroverts. Some people judge more than accept. I suspect you've heard some of the terminology even if you don't know the background of Myers-Briggs.

There is another mechanism, another method I've used that's similar to Myers-Briggs that I find more valuable, that I just really like a lot, and it's called *Conative Connection*. That's a phrase that means "the will to act" and the person who put this work together over the last 40-50 years, Kathy Kolbe, was exploring what makes us want to get up and do something in the morning. You know—not just how we feel about it, our emotional state about it and all of that—but what makes us move; what makes us get up in the morning; what makes us say, "Yeah! I want to do that!"

And Kolbe came up with four dimensions, similar to Myers-Briggs. The first is *Quick Start*—you like to start things, you like new things. Then there's the *Fact Finder*—you are the person who likes to get all the facts before you do something; let's get all the facts. (That reminds me of Joe Friday and Dragnet: "Just the facts, ma'am.") The third one is the *Follow Thru*, people who like to finish things, like to get it made, finished up, and feel accomplished when they do that. The last one is *Implementor*, the person who prefers direct interaction with physical objects or other tangibles. And in each one of these you are measured and the scale is you're either active with it, or you actively resist it, and then some neutral in the middle. So there are these three levels for each dimension. For example, as a *Quick Start*, you either really like to start new things, or you're sort of okay with it but it's not really your thing, or you really don't like to start new things.

I'm an incredibly strong *Quick Start* and I don't like to finish things (low *Follow-Thru*), and when I found that out, it was really fascinating. I read *Conative Connection* many, many years ago, and I literally cried because I was saying to myself, "I can't believe this, I have permission!" After I took the test, I had permission to be how I've been since I was a young child.

I always wanted to see how things worked, so I would take them apart. But putting them back together again? Why would I do that? I took it apart to understand it; I understand it now—why would I want to put it back together again? Whereas other people had the attitude, "You took it all apart… you've got to put it back together again." So I would start a lot of things and I wouldn't finish everything and that was a problem. That was a problem in school; that was a problem in my professional life. It was a problem in lots of places.

Now that I know that's true, what I learned from the Kolbe work is that it's not that I can't finish things—it's that I only have so much of that ability, and if I try to finish everything I will fail. So I reserve finishing to things I think are really important, and a lot of stuff I just don't finish. I'm interested in lots of things. I get interested in something, I'll look into it and then I'm done. And it's frustrating. It's a continual thing I play with because I will over-commit myself. At the start I'm enthusiastic, thinking, "Oh yeah! Let's do this thing, let's do this project!" It's always true for me. But I don't have time in the day to finish everything, so I started learning about myself. A good example: Completing this book has been hard for me.

The question is: What about you, what do you like to do? The kind of work you take on will be different based on the answer to that question. I remember, right after I read *Conative Connection*, I got a call from a company that wanted me to come in and it was great money. I was in my own business at the time and the work was to clean up a bunch of work that somebody else had done, and it was very attractive because of the money. I realized that, because of my acknowledgment of who I am and how I am, that it would be a terrible project for me. I have had projects like that and they are horrible; they are absolutely horrible for me. I tend to just not finish them. And, of course, if you own your own business you really don't want to do that.

So I recommend taking a look at Kolbe. I don't believe it's ever been free on the web, but I think it's worth it. I don't know what the cost is these days but last time I took it, which was some time ago, I think it was $50, and it was worth it. You get a lot of interesting information from them and it's incredibly useful for teams. I have successfully used it to help teams understand whether or not they are balanced. If your team members are all, for example, Quick Starts, it doesn't work very well. You'll start a lot of stuff, but you won't finish things, so you'll want a little bit from the other Conation dimensions on your team.

My first recognition was personally about myself and how I worked, and how I am, and that was incredibly powerful to me. It's made it much easier for me to say "no" to projects that I know I'm not going to do well. So find out what your strength is. Make it easier and only do the kind of work that you know you love and can do better at, and get some help with the other parts. Get somebody else to do part of it with you; pair up with somebody, or something like that.

I remember a project I had. Even though I have been doing software for a long time, I never learned C—it was always too tedious for me. I did plenty of assembly language, but C was just kind of glorified assembly language and I didn't need that. So it's been weird—there was a project where I had to do some C. It wasn't much, but it was some, and I looked at it for a while and went, "Ah, I don't want to do this." I was living in Oregon at the time. I had a friend fly up from California and spend a week with me. It took him two hours to do the work, but we were friends and we visited a lot. He liked it, he got it done really fast, and I didn't have to do it.

So figure out what you like to do and only do that—it's a lot more fun.

Why Software?

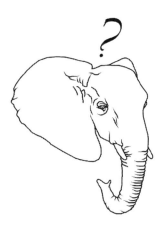

Here's a question: Why are you in software?

I think it is an important question to ask yourself, because it affects how you work, how you think about your work, and how satisfied you are with your work.

I'm a bit of an old hippie, so I believe that one should do things that one loves to do. Now, in certain economic environments that may not always be completely possible. Maybe you can't do something you love to do right now, but in that case it may be even more important for you to pay attention to why you are there and what you are doing, because it will affect how you think about things moving forward and what kind of strides you can make.

There is no right answer to this question; there is only your answer.

But understanding your own answer is very important. Are you just in it for the money? That's a perfectly legitimate reason to be in the software business—or any other business—but it will affect how you live and operate within the industry, and in your career.

Some people may have judgments about money as a motivator. Personally, I don't think it's very sustainable as a primary motivation; I don't think it's a great way to work because you will likely never be satisfied. But maybe it is enough of a reason for you; maybe that's all you need.

Or maybe you have a bigger dream tied to that desire for money. I see a lot of people here in Silicon Valley who have the dream of starting a company and flipping it. That's what they want to do, and there have been a number of people who have done it. That is a perfectly legitimate dream.

For me personally, my love of the mystery of software is what moved me into the field. There was something about software, and software writing and debugging, and making something happen out of almost nothing, that was incredibly cool to me, incredibly stimulating. I started close to the hardware, so using some of that hardware background as well as my mathematical background as I entered the software field made for a situation that was absolutely fascinating to me.

But even when I was very young and wet behind the ears and just starting out in the profession I remember having discussions with my peers saying that what I wanted to do was build software to make people's lives better. That was a serious conversation I would have with others, and with myself, too, and I look back now after more than fifty years in the business and I can say that I've had some success: Some of the project I worked on have made people's lives better. Other projects I worked on, well, I'm not sure they've made people's lives worse, exactly… but who knows?

I do know that this conscious goal has been a driver for me. It has driven me to support simplicity in user interfaces, in getting down to the essence of things, making sure there is not a lot of cruft around the edges of the projects I work on.

Now, the money driver is also there for me, and it has occasionally driven me to stay in the industry, because there have been times when I've gotten tired of software—let me tell you, doing the same thing for fifty years can make you tired! I've even stepped out of the field for small periods of time, and quite frankly the lure of both the money and the mystery and this desire to make things better has always pulled me back in.

Take a look at why you're here. See what you want to do with it, and what you want it to do for you. Is it about the mystery for you, too? Is it making something out of nothing? Is it the conquering of something? Being in charge of something? Is it working with people on a creative team and letting those creative juices flow? Is it making something larger than what you are?

Those are the kinds of questions that may help you decide what kind of work you take on.

Another related question is: If you know what kind of work you are interested in doing, what kind of work would you not do?

At times I have had opportunities to work for companies that I considered unethical. I chose not to work for them. Earlier on in my career I was asked to work on the B1 bomber, which at that point in time was touted as the best project you could possibly hope to get on. And I couldn't do it.

It's important for each of us to know and understand our desires and our limits. Then it is easier to make certain decisions, to get up in the morning and be glad about what we do every day, how we make our living, and to enjoy life.

On Careers

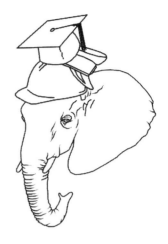

I've had a 50+ year career at this date. I mean, you know, who's counting? How have I managed to do this? I still feel like I'm on the edge. What's going on there? People ask me about this occasionally, so to me it's important because I've been pretty conscious about it over my career. I've thought about how I did this and what I did to make it happen, and part of the answer is that I've been able to recognize the kind of person I am and what I like to do.

As I mentioned before, I am a Kolbe *Quick Start*. I love to start things; new projects; new companies; new challenges.

Each one of us has our own particular blend of characteristics, and that affects what makes us want to do stuff—makes us want to get up in the morning and go to work. I learned fairly early on that doing new things is what I really loved, so I've spent my career making sure that I do a lot of new things. And of course, in a career in computer software, there has been a lot of new stuff over the last 50 years to do, so I've had a lot of good times looking at new things and learning about new things.

My technique for that has been to dive in all the way, and the analogy I like to use is that technology comes in waves. We have all experienced, and we talk about, how AI came in or objects came in or this came in or that came in. And that rate of those things coming in seems to be getting faster and faster. But the thing to remember is that you, as an individual, can't catch it all.

I think of the analogy of surfing. If you are a surfer, the waves come in and you wait until you see a wave you like. You get on it, and then maybe it peters out, maybe it keeps going, but there are other waves that come in. You can't possibly catch every wave. If you try, you don't really get a good ride. And that's what we're here to do as far as I'm concerned: to have a really good ride.

For instance, I got hooked up with objects very early on. And boy, has it been a ride! Likewise I got hooked up with Agile. And computers themselves—when I got started that was a ride nobody had heard about.

So I think the key is getting on to it and then knowing when it's time for you to get out. It may not be time for everybody to get out. There are still people doing COBOL in the world; there are still people using PVCS, but it's been 25 years, I think, since I've touched some of that stuff. So you've got to find out what your place is, what you like, how you operate—to find that place and continue to love what you do. And if you don't love it anymore, you might consider changing what you're doing or doing it a little bit differently.

Afterword

Hi again.

Of course the conversations we have been having really never end. I am sure you could add your own observations and techniques to this collection. I could easily add more myself.

And books must have an end. So here we are. At an end.

I hope that these musings have encouraged you to continue your journey; to be a beginning or even better a continuing exploration on what it is for you to be conscious as a software developer and perhaps more importantly, as a person.

Do listen to your heart!

Jeff
Los Altos, CA
July, 2014

References

Below you will find some references to material mentioned in the book.

Agile Manifesto can be found at http://www.agilemanifesto.org

Agile Testing: A Practical Guide for Testers and Agile Teams
by Lisa Crispin and Janet Gregory)

Conative Connection: Uncovering the Link Between Who You Are and How You Perform
by Kathy Kolbe

MBTI Manual: A Guide to the Development and Use of the Myers-Briggs Type Indicator, 3rd Edition
by Isabel Briggs Myers, Mary H. McCaulley,
Naomi L. Quenk and Allen L. Hammer

Pair Programming Illuminated
by Laurie Williams and Robert Kessler

Software for Your Head: Core Protocols for Creating and Maintaining Shared Vision
by Jim McCarthy and Michele McCarthy

Index

I

implementation architecture 51
Implementor 102
improvement 19
ingredients of an interaction 36
introspection 27

J

Java 59, 62, 63, 66
JOVIAL 60

L

language
  domain specific 64
languages 59
  changing 60
language wars 59
leaarning
  new things 17
learning
  and flow of information 95
  big picture stuff 18
  by doing 17
  by reading 15
  non-technical skills 17
  through trial and error 15
  to learn 15
learning by interacting
  by interacting 16
Lisp 62
listener 35
Lone Ranger 14

M

McCarthy, Jim 29
meditation 99
mental models 41
modeling 16, 56
  languages 42
money
  as a motivator 105
Montana, Joe 27
Myers-Briggs 101
mystery of software 106

14401730R00070

Made in the USA
San Bernardino, CA
26 August 2014